PROCLAIMING THE GOSPEL OF LIFE

EDITED BY

FR RICHARD WHINDER

All documents are published thanks to the generous support of the members of the Catholic Truth Society

CATHOLIC TRUTH SOCIETY
PUBLISHERS TO THE HOLY SEE

CONTENTS

Introduction 3

The role of the priest in promoting the Gospel of Life
    Mgr Ignacio Barreiro 4

Vatican II, Culture and the Gospel of Life
    Aidan Nichols OP 21

Pope Pius XII and the Gospel of Life
    Fr John Saward 35

Challenges and opportunities in pro-life preaching
    Fr Timothy Finigan 53

Contributors 71

Association of Priests for the Gospel of Life. 72

INTRODUCTION

This book reproduces four lectures given to the Association of Priests for the Gospel of Life at their London conferences. It should not be assumed, however, that the contents will only be of interest to a clerical audience: far from it. In his encyclical *Evangelium Vitae* – surely one of the most important documents of his Pontificate – Pope John Paul II stated:

The Gospel of Life is at the heart of Jesus' message. Lovingly received by the Church, it is to be preached with dauntless fidelity as 'good news' to every age and culture (*Evangelium Vitae*, 1).

No believer, then, can be indifferent to this central struggle of our times, and it is hoped that all Catholics of an enquiring mind will find material here to deepen their understanding of this crucial issue and encouragement to redouble their efforts on behalf of the most vulnerable members of society.

In the first lecture Monsignor Ignaccio Barreiro gives us an overview of the worldwide phenomenon of the 'Culture of Death' and outlines the Church's response to it – something he is well placed to do, as Director of the Rome Office of Human Life International. Aidan Nichols OP, one of our most respected theologians, offers us a deeper insight into the contemporary situation in Britain, the particular obstacles we face and the theological and spiritual resources we must use to overcome them. Father John Saward, who is both theologian and parish priest, reminds us that the roots of this crisis go back at least as far as the reign of Pope Pius XII – and gives a timely reminder of the lasting contribution that Pontiff made in resisting the forces of evil. Lastly, Father Timothy Finigan, founder of the Association of Priests for the Gospel of Life, offers a pastoral approach to preaching on this controversial but vital issue. Again, his lecture will repay reading by laity as well as priests – if only to remind the lay faithful to pray constantly that their priests will be given courage to speak out boldly in defence of human life and the truths of the Gospel. To end with the words of *Evangelium Vitae*:

May these words reach all the sons and daughters of the Church! May they reach out to all people of good will who are concerned for the good of every man and woman and for the destiny of the whole of society! (*Evangelium Vitae*, 6).

THE ROLE OF THE PRIEST IN PROMOTING THE GOSPEL OF LIFE

Mgr Ignacio Barreiro

The Context

We live in a society that has turned its back to the truths of Christ and we see the consequences. It is not necessary on this occasion to enter into the details of this situation which is well known to most of you. One of the most troubling consequences of a long process of apostasy is that the culture of death is taking a stronghold in most of the western countries and that the demographic winter is getting colder. We are moving slowly towards a neo-pagan world, that would be far worse that the world that existed before Christianity. A world that was prophesied by George Orwell in his novel *1984*[1] or by Aldous Huxley in *Brave New World*.[2] John Paul II has lamented how the culture of death has entered within the ranks of the Church: he states that "Too often it happens that believers, even those who take active part in the life of the Church, end up by separating their Christian faith from its ethical requirements concerning life, and thus fall into moral subjectivism and certain objectionable ways of acting."[3] At the same time this degeneration and decline is not inexorable, is not predetermined, because it goes against the infinite love of God that strongly desires that all men should come to the knowledge of the truth and be saved.[4] It goes against our Faith in a God who is the Lord of History and we have to be confident that He will raise strong apostles of the Truth who will turn the tide. We have here and there some rays of light that announce that perhaps a new sunrise is dawning.

This situation should spur us to fight on behalf of the culture

---

[1] George Orwell, *1984*, Harcourt Brace Jovanovich, Inc. New York, 1949.
[2] Aldous Huxley, *Brave New World*, Harper & Row, New York, 1969.
[3] John Paul II, *Evangelium Vitae*, 95.
[4] 1 *Tm* 2-4.

of life. The question then that I would like to consider is: what is the role of the priest in promoting the Gospel of Life, and in particular, what is the role of the parish priest? Within the Church we find many charisms, many special vocations, but the mission of the parish priest should not be dominated by any of them, but rather provide a Catholic synthesis of all of them in the measure that they are applicable to parish life. Having a passion for the wholeness of the Catholic Truth, the Blessed Sacrament, the Blessed Virgin Mary, the integral defence of life and many other things that are part and parcel of being a Catholic are not to be considered special charisms. They are just part of being Catholic. In the measure that we foster an authentic Catholic life in our parishes, we will be able to promote the Gospel of Life. But in order to promote the Gospel of Life we need to rekindle the faith. It is true that through his natural reason man can perceive the unique value of human life. However it is also true that man will only value life to the fullest through the gift of faith. Reason leads man to encounter God in the mirror of his creatures, yet it is only revelation that gives us the full measure of our dignity and our hope. So we have to understand that it is very difficult to defend life without defending the fullness of the faith in the same instant. When I speak of the defence of life I am not only talking of defending the unborn child but rather of a series of issues, that obviously start with the protection of the unborn yet go far beyond, such as the struggle against euthanasia in all of its forms or the defence of the family. Remember that the faith is an integrated whole. It is like the wooden planks that form the hull of a sailing ship. If only one of them is missing the ship sinks. Therefore, the presentation of the Faith should be done keeping in mind the resemblance of the children who played either a joyful dance or sung a dirge.[5] Even if the Christian message is an overall message of joy the sorrowful aspects of this message should never be omitted, even if some of them might be considered terribly politically incorrect in our days. On the other hand many of the sorrowful aspects of the saving message are a source of hope,

---

[5] *Mt* 11:16-17.

as for example the Passion and death of Christ. Really the only sad thing about our message is the recognition of the reality of sin, the rebellion of man against God and against himself. As the Archangel Raphael said to Tobias and his son: "But they that commit sin and iniquity are enemies of their own soul."[6]

Preaching the fullness of faith

Today we find in some persons within the Church a tendency of focussing on what are considered the main teachings of the Church. Though this idea is not fundamentally wrong, it runs the risk of ending in a selective presentation of the teachings of the Church. The emphasis on what are considered the main teachings of the Faith can be mixed or even influenced by the contemporary temptations of presenting a mutilated or partial version of the doctrine of the Faith. It is deplorable that many of the so-called Catholic preachers of our days, pass the teachings of the Church through the filter of "what is acceptable for contemporary man." This is just a step away of what a well known planter from Virginia did in building his own gospel by collating in a notebook only what he thought to be truly credible of the Gospel of Christ. Here we should not forget the Christ's warning in the Sermon of the Mountain when he states: "For truly, I say to you, till heaven and earth pass away, not an iota, not a dot, will pass away from the law until all is accomplished. Whoever then relaxes one of the least of these commandments and teaches men so, shall be called the least in the Kingdom of heaven; but he who does them and teaches them shall be called great in the Kingdom of Heaven."[7]

As priests we should take to heart, the Lord's message to the prophet Ezekiel and know the high stakes of failing to preach the fullness of Christ's teaching: "If I say to the wicked man, You shall surely die; and you do not warn him or speak out to dissuade him from his wicked conduct so that he may live: that wicked man shall die for his sin, but I will hold you responsible for his

---

[6] *Tb* 12:10.
[7] *Mt* 5, 18-19.

death."[8] We should keep in mind what is taught in the Decree on the Ministry and Life of Priests of the Second Vatican Council, which perhaps is the best document of that ecclesiastical event. It states that priests, "... should act toward men, not as seeking to please them, but in accord with the demands of Christian doctrine and life. They should teach them and admonish them as beloved sons, according to the words of the Apostle: "Be urgent in season, out of season, reprove, entreat, rebuke in all patience and doctrine" (2 *Tm* 4:2).[9] Against the tendency of making a selective presentation of the doctrine this same document of the twenty first council of the Church, calls upon us to be "unwavering champions of the truth, lest the faithful be carried about by every wind of doctrine."[10] If we look around we can sadly see how many of our fellow Catholics are pushed around by all sort of errors. As Cardinal Ratzinger stated in a brilliant homily the day before he was elected to the See of Peter: "How many winds of doctrine have we known in recent decades, how many ideological currents, how many ways of thinking. The small boat of the thought of many Christians has often been tossed about by these waves – flung from one extreme to another: from Marxism to liberalism, even to libertinism; from collectivism to radical individualism; from atheism to a vague religious mysticism; from agnosticism to syncretism and so forth. Every day new sects spring up, and what St Paul says about human deception and the trickery that strives to entice people into error (cf. *Ep* 4:14) comes true. Today, having a clear faith based on the Creed of the Church is often labeled as fundamentalism. Whereas relativism, that is, letting oneself be "tossed here and there, carried about by every wind of doctrine", seems the only attitude that can cope with modern times. We are building a dictatorship of relativism that does not recognise anything as definitive and whose ultimate goal consists solely of one's own ego and desires."[11]

---

[8] *Ez* 3:18.
[9] *Presbyterorum Ordinis*, n. 6.
[10] *Presbyterorum Ordinis*, n. 9.
[11] Joseph Ratzinger, *Homily at Mass Pro Eligendo Romano Pontifice*, Monday 18th April, 2005.

Many of those errors are the consequence of priests having presented false doctrines. However, in many cases these errors are caused by the fact that for many years the faithful in the different parishes have not heard a clear and articulated presentation of the totality of the faith. They have heard exegeses of the biblical texts that are orthodox at best or simple banalities. Instead the code of Canon Law mandates that in the Sunday homily "the mysteries of the faith and rules of Christian living are to be expounded."[12] Also we should keep in mind, as the Commentary of the Code by the University of Navarre points out, that "A homily, therefore, need not necessarily be focused on the Gospel of the day."[13]

First and foremost we have to strengthen the knowledge of the faith, both at a dogmatic and moral level. The doctrine of the faith has to be presented in an integral way. As a consequence of that we will be able to encourage a fervent spiritual life and the practice of works of charity. Religion cannot be based in a vague feeling nor in a sort of thoughtless solidarity with those who are perceived as disadvantaged. Religion has to be grounded in an objective and precise knowledge. Today we hear a significant amount of talk about the need to encounter Christ and this is fine. But a concrete and recognisable encounter happens through the adherence to a series of concepts about Him, that the Church teaches as the faithful administrator of the treasury of revelation. We can only build an accurate identikit of Christ with the descriptive concepts that the Church gives about him. Thus we cannot find Christ in isolation from the Church.[14] Remember that Christ said: "For whoever does the will of my Father in Heaven is my brother, and sister, and mother."[15] We became members of the Family of God, not through a vague sentimental attachment, but through a concrete observance of His commandments. At the same time we need to be fully aware that the study of the Faith is "not only knowledge of the

---

[12] C.C.L. 767.

[13] *Code of Canon Law Annotated*, University of Navarra – Saint Paul University, Wilson & Lafleur Limitée, Montréal, 1993 p. 504.

[14] John Paul II, *Veritatis Splendor*, 6th August, 1993, n. 7.

[15] *Mt* 12:50.

propositions of the faith in their historical formulation and practical application, but is also always knowledge of them in faith, hope and charity, as Benedict XVI pointed out recently in his address at the Gregorian University.[16]

There is no doubt that we have to increase the catechetical content of our preaching. Most likely it would be a good idea to have some type of homily plan in which, through the duration of the year, we would deal in an orderly way with all the teachings of our Faith, using for this purpose in a particular way the Sundays after Pentecost. We should start from the presentation of God as the creator of all that exists, both of the spiritual and the corporal creatures as it is underlined in the Creed of the IV Lateran Council, the *Firmiter*. We should not ignore the tragedy of the rebellion of the spiritual creatures since it introduced evil into Creation and is closely connected to the fall of our first parents. We can not ignore that those rebel spiritual creatures, due to a mysterious permissive will of God continue to exercise their deleterious influence in the world. This is a reality that has to be presented wisely affirming its horrible existence, but at the same time avoiding that our listeners be overly preoccupied with it. In the rebellion of the angels we see the culture of death, which is a desire of self-destruction, entering into a good creation. As St Thomas Aquinas reminds us, because we were created out of nothingness we always have the temptation of returning to nothingness.[17] The temptation also consists in believing wrongly that it is actually possible to go back to nothingness as a way of liberating us from the pains of the current existence, when, on the contrary, natural reason and revelation teach us that we are going to live for ever – obviously either in perfect beatitude or in total pain and anguish. The man who rebels against the love of God will only find emptiness and anguish which through a merciful disposition of Providence gives him a preview of Hell and might lead to repentance. The doctrine of original sin should be carefully

---

[16] Benedict XVI, Address to the Pontifical Gregorian University, 3rd November, 2006.

[17] St Thomas Aquinas, ST, I, q. 104, a, 3, ad. 1. Charles Journel, *El Mal*, Rialp, Madrid, 1965, p. 140.

explained, especially since it explains our wounded condition. As a consequence we became more aware of our need for grace. This tragedy brought about the merciful intervention of a God who became man, suffered, died and rose again for our salvation. We have to present these events as historical facts that occurred two thousand years ago, but also as events that have a concrete bearing on our lives today. The Christian and in particular the priest are in certain form a continuation of the incarnation of Christ because we continue his mission by trying to live like other Christs. The devotion to Our Lady has to be buttressed with the different magisterial teachings of the Church. I suggest, in particular, that we develop her unique role as co-redemptress and Mediatrix of all graces. Furthermore, I propose that we develop the devotion to the Blessed Virgin Mary as merciful Mother who protects all her children under her mantle. In the pro-life apostolate, it is very valuable to mention her apparition in Guadalupe, Mexico when she appeared to St Juan Diego bearing Jesus in her womb. This a great avocation, when we implore her protection on the child that is unborn.

We should not be too surprised by the wide array of problems that we encounter today in relation to sexual morality. As St Thomas Aquinas reminds us, this is the part of human nature most wounded by original sin.[18] We will have to confront the generalised incorrect opinion that sexual relations between consenting adults are a sort of human right, because apparently no one is hurt. Well, it would be a good idea to explain how they hurt themselves and how they damage society. In the teaching of moral issues related to sexuality we have to start always with God's plan which has granted sexual powers to man so as to use them solely within marriage. We should impart the teachings on marriage, at two levels: Firstly, during our general instructions on the faith, both at the pulpit and in adult formation classes; secondly, insisting on a serious preparation for this sacrament. Regrettably in many places the prenuptial formation process has a very limited and summary scope. Perhaps

---

[18] St Thomas Aquinas, S.T. I-II, q. 83, a. 4.

we might need to tailor our own programs. Defending life from the pulpit would require defending life from conception to its natural conclusion at death. You know well how the movement towards legalising euthanasia is growing in your own country. We need to explain clearly the evil of artificial fertilisation (IVF) and how it leads to the destruction of a significant number of minuscule human beings. We should be careful with the serious problems caused by what is called sexual education. It can do serious damage to children. This type of formation should be left to the parents. We should speak about the virtue of modesty as a response to contemporary fashions. Perhaps the time has come to reintroduce the use of veils in the Church. In the presentation of the teachings we have to be precise, but at the same time prudent, taking into account that there will be children in our congregations. To give an example, if we denounce pornography as we should, we should mention that it is wrong in itself yet also that it leads to other sins. Thus the adult members of the congregation will know what we are talking about.

Contraception

There is a pressing need to present with clarity and precision the teachings on generosity towards life and the evils of contraception. We cannot be authentically pro-life and faithful to the Church if we ignore this issue. They are many organisations and individual parish priests who are ready to denounce the evils of abortion, but regrettably they shy away from the issue of contraception.

It is very important to demonstrate, that the use of artificial means of any type, to control human fertility has always and constantly been condemned by the Church. In 1963, five years before the promulgation of the Papal Encyclical *Humanae Vitae,* two widely respected moral theologians stated: "But we show the binding force, the finality, of the tradition simply by showing that during the last century and a half – a truly crucial period as regards marital morality – the Church has constantly and emphatically taught that contraception is a grave violation of the law of God. For, if the teaching of the Catholic Church on a point so profoundly

Proclaiming the Gospel of Life

and intimately connected with the salvation of millions of souls has been the same over such a long period of time, the inevitable conclusion must be that that teaching is true and unchangeable. Otherwise the Church which God has established to interpret the moral law and to guide souls on the way of salvation would be failing substantially in its divine mission."[19]

After the promulgation of *Humanae Vitae* the following considerations can be made: 1. When the Church proposes a moral teaching that Christians must follow if they are to be saved, the consequence follows that it is a teaching that it must be accepted as certain. 2. The insistent repetition of the teaching contained in *Humanae Vitae*, when it was denied outside the Church and by some voices within the Church, often included the proposition that this is an obligatory teaching, one which every Catholic must hold. 3. The teaching on the immorality of contraception has been proposed as a divinely revealed moral norm. As a consequence it should be held in a definitive way.[20]

As Fr Euteneuer underlines, "Priestly silence about contraception is deadly both to the Church and to our society."[21] The founder of Human Life International, Fr Paul Marx, with his habitual realism, pointed out more than twenty years ago that, "Future generations will wonder why so many Catholic bishops and priests in the West didn't see contraception as a seminal evil and the chief cause of

---

[19] John C. Ford, S.J. and Gerald Kelly, S.J., *Contemporary Moral Theology, v. II, Marriage Questions*, The Newman Press, Westminster, Maryland, 1963, pp. 257.258.

[20] John C. Ford, S.J., Germain Grisez, Joseph Boyle, John Finnis, William E. May, *The Teaching of Humane Vitae A Defense*, Ignatius Press, San Francisco, 1988, pp. 163-164. "4. The Church has always taught the intrinsic evil of contraception, that is, of every marital act intentionally rendered unfruitful. This teaching is to be held as definitive and irreformable. Contraception is gravely opposed to marital chastity; it is contrary to the good of the transmission of life (the procreative aspect of matrimony), and to the reciprocal self-giving of the spouses (the unitive aspect of matrimony); it harms true love and denies the sovereign role of God in the transmission of human life." Pontifical Council for the Family, *Vademecum for Confessors Concerning some Aspects of Morality of Conjugal Life*, 12th February, 1997.

[21] Fr Thomas J. Euteneuer, *Clerical Contraception*, in Spirit & Life, Human Life International e-Newsletter, vol 1., Number 36, Friday 6th October, 2006.

the Church's swift decline."[22] We have to see contraception as a form of blatant rebellion against God, because the couple that places knowingly an obstacle to conception in some ways is putting an end to the continuation of creation. It is a rejection of God's sovereignty over marriage and a refusal to obey the Lord's command to "be fruitful and multiply" which is a fundamental and permanent commandment of God to our first parents. So we have to be ready to admonish couples that contraception or sterilisation are mortal sins and should prevent a couple using contraception or sterilisation from receiving communion.

In speaking of the evils of contraception, first and foremost we have to present supernatural arguments, but following a tradition of common sense we should also use natural arguments against this evil. At a supernatural level we have to reflect on how all human persons receive a call from God to be members of the Kingdom of Heaven, through the living of a good life on earth. The married couple receives their call to sanctification as co-creators with God and administrators of the gift of Life. They should be asked to meditate on the fact that they have freely received the gift of life from a loving God and that they have the responsibility of sharing this gift, generating life. They should be induced to ponder as well on how their generosity would lead to the begetting of new members for the Heavenly Kingdom. Their generosity with life will lead perhaps to the begetting of great apostles of the Kingdom of God, men or women of great talent and holiness that would be able to reverse the current trend of decay of the world. As Fr Euteneuer rightly remarks, priests who are silent about the teaching on contraception also forget two very important things: first, priestly vocations generally come from large families. Failure to preach openness to life and generosity with children has a direct effect on how many men will be standing in the front lines with us later on. Being silent about this teaching has the same effect as contracepting the marital act: sterility. The persistent sterility of priestly vocations is caused to a large extent by priests who are

---

[22] Quoted by Fr Euteneuer, in the above mentioned article.

Proclaiming the Gospel of Life

silent about the plague of contraception among the laity and forget that their own vocations are the result of their parents' generosity with life. Overworked and lonely priests will be reaping the fruits of their silence on contraception for a long time.

Secondly, priestly silence about contraception has eternal consequences. The price of that silence is the loss of souls. Contracepting men and women who are not warned of their sin and who therefore do not repent risk damnation, and this is a scandal of immense proportions. Perhaps the only danger of greater consequence is the danger to the priests themselves who don't fulfil their responsibilities: they risk their own salvation because in the end they will be held accountable for not preaching the Church's full message "in season and out of season."

At a border area between the supernatural and natural level we can demonstrate that couples who follow the teachings of the Church on the rightful use of marriage have a stronger likelihood of having a happy marriage and remaining united until death than couples who act against the Law of God. Comprehensive studies demonstrate that nearly *one-half* of all marriages now taking place in the United States will end in divorce, annulment or separation.[23] Contrast this abysmal failure rate with that of married couples who use natural family planning: The divorce/separation rate among these couples is *less than one in eight.*[24]

At a natural level, we have ample scientific evidence that demonstrates the connection between abortion and different forms of contraception with an increased risk of breast and womb cancer.[25] A high percentage of women have taken the Pill for some time in their lives, but few of them are aware that the Pill is in fact classified as a "group-one carcinogen" by the International

---

[23] United States Department of Commerce, Bureau of the Census. *Statistical Abstract of the United States*, 1999. Washington, D.C.: U.S. Government Printing Office, 1999. Table 91, "Live Births, Deaths, Marriages and Divorces: 1950 to 1997."

[24] Research done by Dr. Brian Clowes of HLI through contacts with 14 major national NFP groups and leaders. The number shown is the average (the range is from 0.6 percent to 20 percent). The lowest figure quoted is 0.6 percent, from Nona Aguilar's book *The New No-Pill No-Risk Birth Control* (New York: Rawson Associates), 1986, page 188.

[25] Chris Kahlenborn, MD, *Breast Cancer – Its Link to Abortion and the Birth Control Pill*, One More Soul, Dayton, 2000.

Agency for Research on Cancer in 2005.[26] We have a very recent study, written by Drs. Chris Kahleborn, Francesmary Modugno, Douglas M. Potter, and Walter B. Severs and published in the October 2006 journal of the Mayo Clinic, that demonstrates that the use of oral contraceptives is a risk factor for Pre-menopausal breast Cancer. In this study it is amply demonstrated that the use of oral contraceptives is linked with a measurable and statistically significant association with pre-menopausal breast cancer. The risk association is 44% over a baseline of women having been pregnant took Oral Contraceptives prior to their first pregnancy.[27]

Television

TV is found everywhere. More so, it has become normal for many middle class families to own several sets. It is a piece of technology that is voluntarily inserted into the heart of our homes that is a vehicle for anti-Catholic agendas and pagan ideologies that use this medium to distort our sense of reality and entertain us into moral complacency at best. At worst the TV programs or even the publicity can be an occasion of sin. This piece of equipment has to be recognised as the "most probable" prime cause for making an immoral home environment that can accept abortion.[28] But it will be reductive to focus only on the evils of TV with regards to sexual morality. TV is constantly presenting a world view, a conception of man and society that in most cases is directly opposite to the Catholic view of reality. It influences the way in which we think and see reality in many subtle ways with images that bypass the rational function. So my advice is to liberate ourselves of the tyranny of this foreign intruder and remove the televisions from our homes. I know that for many people it will be hard to free themselves from this addiction, but it can done, even gradually by

---

[26] Andrea Mrozek, *Use with caution: Pink ribbons are well and good. But why aren't people talking about the link between the pill and breast cancer?*, National Post, Canada, Friday October 20, 2006.

[27] www.polycarp.org.

[28] Father Frank Poncelet, *Television: Prelude to Chaos*, The Neuman Press, Long Prairie, Minnesota, no date, p. 32.

a process of TV fasting. Some years ago for Lent, John Paul II advised the faithful to fast from TV.[29] If we expel this box from our homes we will have more time to increase the dialogue within the family, we will have more time for reading, praying and even to indulge into useful hobbies.

The Four Last Things

The reality of the four last things should be expounded. We live in a society that masks or tries to ignore the anguishing reality of death. We have to remove this stupid veil and confront reality. For this reason I think that, among other things, we should return to the use of dark vestments for requiem masses. The last but not least of the corporal works of mercy is to bury the dead. Perhaps one of the works of charity that our parishes might want to consider is to help the families, who lack the financial means for a proper burial, to bury their dead in decent cemeteries and thus avoid the problematic practice of cremation. The personal judgment which all of us will undergo in the moment after death will have to be presented with all its stark reality. Then the great alternatives will have to be presented, Heaven or Hell. Obviously the nature of Heaven with all its greatness escapes our weak minds, but revelation and the works of many saints grant us some elements to build a convincing presentation. We should enkindle the desire to go to Heaven. As St Thomas Aquinas explains we cannot have a desire for something if we do not have some sort of knowledge of it first. We build the knowledge of Heaven through a rational dogmatic presentation but also we can point to some experiences that we have on this earth that are foretastes of this reality. A well celebrated liturgy should give us some sort of foretaste of Heaven. The fear of Hell has to be strengthened with precision. In some ways it is easier to speak about Hell. Many persons have experiences that relate to that horrible state. Purgatory, as an experience that hopefully most of us will have to undergo, should be explained. Two reasons make necessary the explanation of this state of purification, of the duty in justice

---

[29] John Paul II, Angelus on St Peter's Square on the III Sunday of Lent, 10th March, 1996.

to pray for the souls in purgatory and the doctrine of indulgences. We should demonstrate how every sin leads to two consequences: 1.) The guilt incurred by the sinner through his actions, that can be forgiven through a good confession. 2. The punishment which is the consequence of sin. This punishment can be eternal if the sinner dies without repentance or temporal, to be expiated in Purgatory, if he dies repentant and has not atoned this punishment through sufficient acts of charity, penance and gaining indulgences during his lifetime. This understanding of the consequences of sin has serious implications in the pro-life apostolate. When someone confesses a sin against life we need to impose an appropriate and serious penance that would have two functions: 1. Underline the gravity of the sin. 2. Assist the person in purging the temporal punishment due to that sin. In the current climate of laxity, in recent years there has been a tendency to impose only symbolic penances. We have to understand though, that a real penance will serve the penitent in many ways to understand that through this penance he will repair in a partial way the sin he has committed, obviously without entering into the theology of this matter. We know that most of this weight of sin is repaired by the blood that Christ shed in His passion.

Faith, Hope and Charity

The theological virtues of Faith, Hope and Charity should be visited and revisited in many ways. Faith is seen today as a vague adherence to God and less as a concrete and living knowledge of the specific truths that are presented to us by the Church. We have to explain in season and out of season how faith is a supernatural virtue that leads to the full adherence to the objective teachings of the Church. The two-fold meaning of the virtue of Hope has to be set clear: first the hope that the promises of Christ with regards to Heavenly Kingdom will be fulfilled and second, that the Lord will grant us all the supernatural and natural assistance that we need to fulfil our duties on earth. Charity perhaps is a very much distorted and banalised virtue in our days. Charity has to be seen first and foremost as the desire for the good of those around us, and the main good we should desire for them is their salvation. Subordinated to this desire we should engage in corporal works of mercy for the ones that the Lord places around us, without ever forgetting the principal importance of the spiritual works of mercy.

Promoting the Spiritual Life

In promoting the spiritual life, the starting point, we should celebrate the sacred liturgy in a way that shows that we truly believe in the real presence of the Lord at the Holy Sacrifice of the Mass. We have to recommend a faithful and frequent reception of the Sacraments of Penance and its connection with a salutary participation at the Holy Sacrifice of the Mass. The Sacrament of Penance not only purifies our souls of all the sins that we could have committed, but allows us also to receive a flow of actual graces that will strengthen our life. The question that we need to answer is how are we Catholics going to feel the need to spread the gospel of life if we do not respect appropriately the source and model of all life, which is present in our midst in the Blessed Sacrament of the Altar.

More than thirty years ago Wilhelmsen showed how "The empty womb stripped of its child by an abortionist is analogous to the empty altar stripped of its God by the theological abortionist – the man who either denies, or, what is more frequent, ignores or plays down the Real presence of Our Lord Jesus Christ in the Sacrifice of the Mass and in the Blessed sacrament of the Altar."[30]

There is a fundamental link between the Holy Sacrifice of the Mass and our pro-life apostolate. The life giving presence of Christ in the Eucharist is the consequence of the unique sacrifice that happened on Calvary and of the un-bloody sacrifice of a single Mass. As a consequence of both sacrifices Christ is present in the tabernacle. In the same way, life and the culture of life will be again present in the midst of our decaying societies as a consequence of our sacrifices. But if we celebrate liturgies that tend to obscure and hide away the sacrificial nature of the Mass, the drive to make

---

[30] Frederick D. Wilhelmsen, *Empty Womb Empty Altar*, Latin Mass Magazine, v. 2, n. 2, April-March 1993, p. 41.

sacrifices to defend the faith might run the risk of dwindling, and the motivation to do the necessary efforts and sacrifices for raising and educating children might dry down.

Besides a respectful celebration of the liturgy the adoration of the Blessed Sacrament should be encouraged and facilitated to the outmost. Here we have the permanent presence of God on earth. Experience has shown that a parish that practices this most central spiritual action will have its faith re-enkindled and many graces will descend upon a congregation that is kneeling in silent adoration of the Lord. As Benedict XVI recently underlined we have to re-discover in the Eucharistic Sacrament the source of our own hope.[31] It should be encouraged that the faithful should be in silent adoration before the Lord. For some of the faithful it might be difficult to be in silent adoration, so I suggest that in our programs of adult formation we should explain how to meditate. Marian devotions need to be promoted, in particular the development of a confidence in the all powerful intercession of Our Lady as Merciful Mother of all the Christians that always keep us under the protection of her mantle.

Works of Charity

The works of charity can be various, but the pro-life apostolate should take pride of place. The pro-life work is at the same time a spiritual and a physical work of mercy. It is spiritual because we are concerned with the salvation of the woman and her child that she is risking to kill with the abortion. It is physical, because we should give a woman in that condition, all the necessary support so that she should be able to bring to completion an unwanted or unplanned pregnancy which in most cases will be the fruit of an immoral act. The spiritual aspect of our apostolate should take preponderance, so we have to make a serious effort to bring about the conversion of the woman who is at risk.

Another suggestion might be to revive the Conference of St

---

[31] Benedict XVI, *Address to the Participants in the Plenary Assembly of the Pontifical Committee for the International Eucharistic Congress*, 9th November.

Vincent de Paul or a similar institution where laymen could organise themselves to visit the parish. Perhaps in the parishes in England you will not be able to find many families or persons who are physically destitute. But certainly if we start doing some parish visitation we will find families who have all sorts of problems and whom perhaps we might be able to help in many different ways. We might find many lonely persons whom we could encourage to become part of different parish groups.

Conclusions

Before I conclude I would like to finish with a note of hope, a hope that is based both in reason and nature and in the supernatural hope that we all have as Christians. It is not a position of optimism, because an optimist is a happy fool in the same way that a pessimist is a sad fool. I believe that the denial of life, both the will to avoid the coming about of natural life and the parallel and terrifying other side of the coin, which is euthanasia, like the partial and reductive presentation of the faith are unnatural and they are going to pass away. First and foremost, because as St Thomas Aquinas stated many times, an unnatural situation can not last for ever because there is nothing more unnatural than denying life or denying the truth, either through a falsification of the truth or through a partial presentation. Second, because the sin of man can never stop the saving action of God, which rather sooner than later will rise again, unimpeded by the errors and follies of mankind. In the meantime we have to wait and fight the good battle, with the same attitude of Cardinal Stepinac who in the bad times that God called him to be a bishop, used as his motto in his coat of arms *"In Te, Domine, speravi."* (In you my Lord a place my hope).[32] I deeply believe that in a not distant future the desire for truth and for life will be enkindled again in the minds and hearts of man. They will receive and practice the Truth and as consequence they will be totally committed to defend life.

---

[32] Gaimpaolo Mattei, *Il Cardinale Alojsije Stepinac – Una vita eroica nella testimoniansa di quanti con lui sono stati vittime della persecuzione nella Jugoslavia comunista,* Quaderni de "L'Osservatore Romano" Città del Vaticano, 1999, p. 86.

VATICAN II, CULTURE AND THE GOSPEL OF LIFE

Aidan Nichols OP

Introduction

An association of priests for the gospel of life is not only a beautiful idea in the Church at any time, but also an especially necessary one in the Church in our country at the present time. It is principally necessary owing to the moral wasteland into which England has fallen. But it is necessary in a secondary way because when considering the moral condition of culture members of the Church have not always sent out clear signals to the people of our day.

So in my introduction I would like to say a word about these two somewhat inter-connected states of affairs. First, what I call, with apologies to T.S. Eliot, the wasteland. How can we characterise the moral culture which surrounds us? It is a culture of individual rights coexisting with a high degree of scepticism about the distinction between right and wrong, and a retreat from responsibility. To a degree it already was these things in Eliot's day, but the degree in question has since been grossly maximised. A sample of instances of contemporary moral anarchy pertinent to life-issues suggests how much. By the year 2020 on present trends in the United Kingdom, married couples will be a minority, and one in three people will be living alone – with all the implications that must have for the procreation and nurture of children. Again: it can be reported with no expectation of outrage that a lesbian couple practising self-insemination before breaking up their partnership had two Do-It-Yourself babies using a pickle jar and syringe, and another similar couple purchased the frozen sperm of a stranger via the Internet.[33] Yet again: to test the potential curative powers of human embryonic stem cells, biologists are currently seeking to inject them into laboratory animals so that, to take two examples of proposed experiments by scientists in good standing in their

---

[33] I take these examples from David Selbourne's *Moral Evasion* (London 1998), pp. 3-8.

profession, a mouse might have a brain made up entirely of human cells, a chimpanzee might have a human mid-brain spliced into its own with the consequence, it is predicted, that though unable to talk, it would be able to laugh or at least sob.[34] Faced with the issues raised by such a sampling of scenarios and others of less directly pro-life concern, there can be noted, reports the ethical commentator David Selbourne, eleven types of evasive argument, which he lists as follows: the notion that 'there is nothing you can do about it, or not much'; the idea that 'it has never been any different'; the proposition that 'there is no quick fix' for a given ethical dilemma; the excuse that 'this is the price of a free society'; the call that 'everything is changing and you must move with the tide'; the cliché that 'it is no use turning the clock back'; the insistence that a problem is 'much more complex than you think'; the alibi that a problem is 'beyond the reach of law'; the objection that 'you are focusing on the wrong issue'; the defence that 'people in glass houses shouldn't....', and, basest of all, since 'everyone does it, or most-people-do', how can you object?[35]

As Selbourne points out, the overall effect of these evasions is to paralyse debate, but if the arguer persist he or she will as likely as not be dismissed as a 'moral crusader', a 'moral authoritarian;, a 'puritan', or, as he puts it, 'the old standby – "right-wing"'.[36] As the Chief Rabbi of Great Britain has put it:

> A view has slowly coalesced that the individual makes choices and the State deals with the consequences of those choices without passing judgment. Order is guaranteed [he goes on] by the police, education by the national curriculum, welfare by government agencies. Morality – the acquisition of habits of self-restraint – has become redundant.[37]

What, then, about my second introductory motif, the sending-out of

---

[34] J. Shreeve, 'The Other Stem-Cell Debate', *The New York Times*, 10th April, 2005, pp. 41-47.

[35] D. Selbourne, *Moral Evasion*, op. cit., pp. 27-42.

[36] Ibid., pp. 19-24.

[37] J. Sacks, 'Therapy instead of Morality', *The Times*, 5th July 1996.

signals by Catholics nationally to their non-Catholic contemporaries about the moral scene? I am not thinking here of official statements – by 2004 at any rate, with the Catholic Bishops Conference booklet *Cherishing Life*, these had become savvy – but of unofficial attitudes among a tranche of ordinary laity and clergy, and of the not-so-ordinary would-be opinion-formers in the media. As so often, those attitudes were affected by the confusion into which Catholic teaching fell in England, if not only here, in the immediate aftermath of the Council, as also by the desire, in a national church (if the phrase may be allowed) emerging from the ghetto to capture the benevolence of the wider public. I think it is fair to say that from the later 1960s on such response frequently took the form of what might be called 'attenuated existentialism'.

Attenuated existentialism, while not necessarily denying in a formal way the reality of an abiding human nature, or the ethical demands integral to the order of grace, nonetheless emphasised chiefly the sincerity of those involved in moral decision-making, and the authenticity of decisions made according to personal conscience. When people say, 'But it's my right', they are, it was and is felt, staking out a proper claim to due autonomy which should be respected, whatever the so-called 'Yuck factor' involved. The Church, after all, following the example of her Master, should not sit in judgment on the world, but serve it, statements which can claim some corroboration from the Pastoral Constitution of the Second Vatican Council on the Church in the Modern World, *Gaudium et Spes*, since its preface ends with more or less exactly those words.

I shall be looking at some strengths and weaknesses of that document in our perspective in a moment. But let me for now contrast what I have called the 'attenuated existentialism' of secular-minded Catholic liberalism with two citations coming from (as they say) somewhere very different. The first is taken from the writings of the historian of philosophy Etienne Gilson, and considers one crucial theme already touched on, namely conscience: Besides being bound to obey our conscience [wrote Gilson], we are also bound, whenever an error of judgment is to be feared, to criticise it, and to replace a bad conscience by a better.[38]

The second citation is pertinent to the wider question of Church strategy, and it has no less a source than the founder of *The Tablet*, Frederick Lucas. Lucas asked:

> What principles can beget and develop enthusiasm for the cause of the Church?... Is it by acting so as to satisfy and please the half-religious, the indifferent, the careless, the timid, that men can ever create religious (or other) enthusiasm? Is it by truckling to fears, and doubts, and deficient energy? Was it by half-measures that St Paul inspired his followers with a willingness to die? Was it by meeting the wisdom of the world half-way that Hildebrand saved the Church from its oppressors? [And he replied to his own questions:] We think not.[39]

The hermeneutic of renewal in continuity

My next section is entitled 'the hermeneutic of renewal in continuity'. I felt moderately certain that this phrase will be more than a polysyllabic exotic to members of the Association of Priests for the Gospel of Life. It was in fact popularised (if that is indeed the word) by the present pope in an address to the Roman Curia on the 40th anniversary of the conclusion of the Second Vatican Council: 22nd December, 2005. That address sought to define one way of reading the texts of that Council as the only way fully acceptable within the context of Catholic tradition. But, by its emphasis on continuity rather than rupture as the hallmark of the Spirit's guidance in Tradition (in 'tradition' there a capital T is called for), Benedict's speech also exemplified a wider mind-set in Christian thinking. In some pithy words of G.K. Chesterton: [r]eal development is not leaving things behind, as on a road, but drawing life from them, as from a root.[40]

Treating the Conciliar moment as one of reform not revolution,

---

[38] E. Gilson, *The Spirit of Medieval Philosophy* (Et New York 1940), pp. 352-353.

[39] E. Lucas, *The Life of Frederick Lucas*, M. P. (London 1886), I. p. 279.

[40] G. K. Chesterton, *The Victorian Age in Literature* (London 1925), p. 12.

Benedict XVI spoke of the proper method of appropriating the Conciliar texts as a hermeneutic suited to such reform, which implies, as he put it: renewal in the continuity of the one subject-Church that the Lord has given to us. She is a subject that increases in time and develops; yet always remaining the same, the one subject of the journeying People of God.

Oddly enough, the pope was, I think, more eloquent or at any rate more fulsome on the topic of the hermeneutic of discontinuity which he was opposing. Typically, he declared, the practititioners of such a hermeneutic claim that the texts of the Council are the result of compromises in which, to reach unanimity, it was found necessary to keep and reconfirm many old things that are now pointless. However, the true spirit of the Council is not [it was alleged] to be found in these compromises but instead in the impulses toward the new that are contained in the texts. These innovations alone were supposed to represent the true spirit of the Council, and starting from and in conformity with them, it would be possible to move ahead. Precisely because the texts would only imperfectly reflect the true spirit of the Council and its newness, it would be necessary to go courageously beyond the texts and make room for the newness in which the Council's deepest intention would be expressed, even if it were still vague. In a word: it would be necessary not to follow the texts of the Council but its spirit. In this way, obviously [the pope argued], a vast margin was left open for the question on how this spirit should subsequently be defined and room was consequently made for every whim.

All this, commented the pope, exemplified a failure to grasp the nature of the conciliar process. An ecumenical Council is not a constituent assembly that, as he put it, 'eliminates an old constitution and creates a new one'. As he concluded:

> The Fathers [i.e. the bishops in Council] had no such mandate and no one had ever given them one; nor could anyone have given them one because the essential constitution of the Church comes from the lord and was given to us so that we might attain eternal life and, starting from this perspective, be able to illuminate life

in time and time itself.[41]

I think it is worth reminding ourselves of this important interpretative principle, even at the expense of so lengthy a citation, since in order to claim for the proclamation of the Gospel of life a non-ambiguous mandate in the documents of the Council, we need to be able to clear away the misunderstanding whereby what I termed 'attenuated existentialism' could stand as a legitimate expression of Vatican II's attitude towards moral culture at large.

Am I setting up here a straw man to be too easily knocked down? Has anyone actually held that 'attenuated existentialism' is the implicit recommended stance towards other persons in civil society of the Church at Vatican II? Well, no – though that is partly because I've only just come up with the expression! What has been discerned in the small or not so small print of *Gaudium et spes* is, however, two claims which, taken together, would generate an an attitude very much like the one I have described. Stating these two claims takes us into the meat of the Pastoral Constitution. Responding to them on the basis of a fuller reading of the Conciliar text, against the backcloth of Tradition with, in the foreground, some declarations of the post-Conciliar papal magisterium in mind, will help us, I hope, to answer convincingly the claim that what you are doing in this association may represent the priorities of Karol Wojtyla and his personal theological preoccupation with, in his own phrase, the 'culture of death' but it does not have much to do with the last General Council of the Church.

Reading 'Gaudium et spes'

So on to my next section: 'Reading *Gaudium et spes*'. The two claims made by interpreters of the Pastoral Constitution which, once read in tandem, could appear to licence attenuated existentialism are these. First, at certain points – such as paragraphs 36 and 59 – *Gaudium et spes* asserts the autonomy vis-à-vis the Church of the

---
[41] Benedict XVI, 'Ad Romanam Curiam ob omina natalicia', *Acta Apostolicae Sedis* XCIII (6th January 2006), pp. 40-53.

secular sciences, of human culture, and of civil society at large. While some commentators, like the contributors to the Alberigo *History of Vatican II* reacted with at any rate equanimity,[42] others, like Dr Tracey Rowland of the John Paul II Institute in Melbourne, were absolutely aghast.[43] Historians can note in an eirenic kind of way that, doubtless, many of the bishops were seeking to reassure scientists, artists, professionals and politicians that the Church after the Council would not wish to maintain or re-institute a heavy-handed or overbearing style of ecclesiastical regime. But the question remains, Do such presentational concerns suffice to explain the wording of what are, after all, doctrinal texts, or should one say, as one reader of Rowland's book puts it:

that the Council fathers overreacted to the threat of integralism because they had already grown weary of the baggage of the Church's tradition in general and desired to throw off some of the weight and ballast of the past in order to embrace a liberal order for which many of them had deep sympathies.[44]

In point of fact, Rowland does not think that things were that bad. But she does think that by embracing at certain points of their text notions of moral and cultural autonomy the Council fathers were extraordinarily naïve. They failed to realise that, in the way modern culture has developed, that culture is not neutral vis-à-vis the *bona recepta*, the 'received goods' – truths, values, practices – of Catholic

---

[42] N. Tanner, 'Chapter V: The Church in the World (*Ecclesia ad extra*). I. Church and World', in *History of Vatican II, Volume IV: Church as Communion: Third Period and Intersession, September 1964-September 1965*, ed. G. Alberigo, English version ed. J. A. Komonchak (Maryknoll, NY, and Leuven 2003), pp. 269-330; G. Routhier, 'Finishing the Work Begun: the Trying Experience of the Fourth Period. IIB. 'Schema XII', *History of Vatican II, Volume V. The Council and the Transition. The Fourth Period and the End of the Council, September 1965-December 1965* (Maryknoll, NY, and Leuven 2006), pp. 122-177; P. Hünermann, 'The Final Weeks of the Council. III. Final Work on *Gaudium et spes*', ibid., pp. 386-427.

[43] T. Rowland, *Culture and the Thomist Tradition. After Vatican II* (London and New York 2003), especially pp. 11-34.

[44] L. S. Chapp, 'The Retrieval of *Gaudium et Spes:* A Comparison of Rowland and Balthasar', *Nova et Vetera* 3. 1 (2005), pp. 118-146, and here at p. 131.

Christianity. Far less is it likely to serve as a *praeparatio evangelica* in the way classical culture did. Unfortunately, statements can also be found – not, thank goodness, uniformly – from the popes of the Council which give the impression that, as Professor Larry Chapp of DeSales University, Pennsylvania, has it, modern culture might embody in a secular way

> many of the same truths held by the Church in a more theological modality, thus opening the door to a new level of cooperation between the secular and ecclesiological realms, as well as implying a general approval for the manner in which modern secularism had developed culturally.[45]

The first ground, then, for asserting a basis for attenuated existentialism in the Pastoral Constitution lies in the licence it gives at various points to the sciences, culture and society in general to develop in their own fashion in fulfilment of their rightful claims to autonomy. As early as 1969 one Joseph Ratzinger could be found deploring what he deemed the Pelagian overtones of such autonomy discourse. Actually, what he said was rather stronger than that: *Gaudium et spes* was marred by '*eine geradezu pelagianische Terminologie*' – a thoroughly Pelagian terminology.[46] Certainly the language used by the Council fathers was a far cry from John Paul II's reported practice in *ad limina* visits of asking bishops what they were doing to 'change culture' in their countries.

The second ground for asserting such a basis for attenuated existentialism is connected with the issue of the manner in which modern secularism has developed culturally. And this has to do not so much with particular brief paragraphs, or the odd sentence, in the document. It concerns, rather its overall theological framework which, it is alleged, considers man to be first and foremost the creative animal destined for global dominion, whose dignity lies in his capacity to imitate, and indeed participate in, the creativity of

---

[45] Ibid., p. 124.
[46] In H. Vorgrimler (ed.), *Commentary on the Documents of Vatican II. V. Pastoral Constitution on the Church in the Modern World* (Et New York 1969), p. 332.

God by achieving effective mastery over the world – thus paragraph 12 of *Gaudium et spes* which is the Constitution's initial statement about the dignity of human persons.

Put that together with the occasional assertions about the autonomy of the secular and what might we get? Is not what we might get the idea that human intervention in the created order through the ingenuity of technology, including medical technology, is in and of itself (no further questions asked) an example of human beings acting exactly as they should, namely, in the image of God who is absolute and intrinsic creativity as distinct from our contingent and mediated creativity? In that case, the message of the text, is, not to put too fine a point on it, the message of the serpent in the Garden: *sicut dii eritis*, 'Ye shall be as gods'. It is the anthropological error known to students of European literature as Prometheanism from the Greek hero Prometheus who stole fire from the gods and brought it down to earth. If we follow this view of the overall theological framework in *Gaudium et Spes* – which means in terms of the text privileging the rather theistic-sounding, as distinct from Trinitarian, statement in paragraph 12 over a densely Christological correlative statement in paragraph 22, then, to cite Chapp again:

> The emphasis will be on human doing and can lead, ironically, to an almost Promethean spirituality that views it as our theological imperative to take on duties that have traditionally been ascribed to the agency of God – as seen for example in the instrumentalisation of human life in abortion and embryo research – all justified by liberal Christians on the grounds that God has blessed us with rationality and it is now our duty to creatively subdue the world by bringing everything, including human life itself, under the umbrella of the technological imperative.[47]

It was, I think I am correct in saying, John Paul II, in his first encyclical, *Redemptor Hominis,* who was the first to highlight the

---
[47] Ibid., p. 128.

importance, rather, of the alternative *imago Dei* doctrine in *Gaudium et spes*, the Christologically ordered one, as a more adequate key, against the background of Tradition, to the message of the Pastoral Constitution as a whole. But, taking up this cue, it was a Washington theologian, David Schindler, a Balthasarian and the editor of the English-language version of the journal *Communio*, who most fully drew out the implications – crucially in an important article in *Communio* for 1996,[48] but at greater length in his book of the same year, *Heart of the World* whose sub-title includes, significantly, the words 'liberalism and liberation'.[49] Schindler's claim was that if, in the light of *Gaudium et spes* 22, one adopts for reading the document – and for doctrine at large – a more Christologically oriented anthropology, then the primary constitutive act of human agency shifts from one of active creativity to one of an active receptivity of creation: active receptivity of creation as sheer gift. If I am the image of God by reference to the Trinitarian Son, then *receiving* – as the Son does from the Father – is more crucial for me, more primordial (in Schindler's term, more *constitutive*) than any creative action I might perform. Indeed, it is, wrote Schindler, the 'inner-anterior condition of all creaturely doing and making'.[50] This 'receiving' in my case, as an image of *the* Image, the Son, means receiving first and foremost from God in his creation of myself. By my nature I am not a god. I am not even like unto a god. Instead, I am a gift. Such awareness of the "giftedness" of existence will naturally extend beyond 'mere gratitude for my own existence into an appreciation of the giftedness of the existence of the "other"'. This alternative anthropology will, therefore, appropriately issue in an 'ethic of love rather than one of manipulative domination'.[51]

In those last words we are coming within hailing distance of a 'Gospel of life', but what I want us to draw from this debate is also

---

[48] 'Christology and the *imago Dei*: Interpreting *Gaudium et Spes*', *Communio* 23 (1996), pp. 156-184.

[49] *Heart of the Word, Center of the Church. Communio Ecclesiology, Liberalism and Liberation* (Edinburgh 1996).

[50] Ibid., p. xv.

[51] L. Chapp, 'The Retrieval of *Gaudium et spes*', art. cit., pp. 128-129.

an inkling of how an emphasis on the potency of the human person, acting in the place of the Creator, especially where that action has access to modern technology, notably medical technology, could easily – and disastrously – fuse with an emphasis on autonomy – scientific autonomy, cultural autonomy, civil autonomy – to produce precisely an ethic of manipulative domination totally untutored by the teaching and ethos of the Church, and totally untutored, above all, by her great narrative of how her Lord and Master became our redeemer in the womb of blessed Mary and manifested his power of love at its uttermost in his physical weakness when dying on the Cross – with all the pregnant implications these Christological episodes have for the issues of abortion and euthanasia. It is not hard to see how, at a less sophisticated conceptual level, and tempered no doubt by habitual charity, what ordinary Church people drew from such a fusion of Prometheanism and autonomy-thinking was some version of what I've been terming 'attenuated existentialism', itself a mild form of the overall stance of contemporary modernity in the secular setting.

For many people the controversy aroused by *Humanae Vitae* took this hitherto fitfully crystallising attitude and fixed it in amber. The alternative to allowing what were really secular mores some ecclesial space was just too provocative, too painful, too divisive. Any search for common ground with secular modernity can only be, however, a highly ambiguous good for the Church, simply because if the foundational principle of that modernity is Promethean autonomy (and this seems likely) then such modernity can only be *au fond* anti-Christian. It's hardly surprising that in the contemporary West the view that religion should be in this or that regard determinative of secular activities has come to be deemed, as Cardinal Avery Dulles has stated, no better than fanaticism.[52] Nor does that opinion simply postdate '9/11'.

So far what I've said may give the impression that *Gaudium et spes* is at least equally amenable to interpretations that point towards and away from classical Christianity – or maybe is, taken

---

[52] A. Dulles, 'Orthodoxy and Social Change', *America* 178. 21 (1998), p. 10.

neat, more susceptible than not to a discontinuous or revolutionary hermeneutic. In the areas that concern us, such a hermeneutic would, in context, enfeeble Gospel of life imperatives by defining human dignity in the typically Liberal terms of autonomy of choice: 'pro-choice' as the phrase has it. In that case, the list of anti-life infamies in paragraph 27 of the Constitution would be an example of what pope Benedict in his 2005 address called standard reiterations of ancient teaching which pale into insignificance compared with the innovatory impulses in the text which are what is really interesting about it. Despite the weaknesses in *Gaudium et spes* (I take it we have gone beyond the stage of Conciliar fundamentalism which can admit no flaws at all in the Council's wording), that is hardly the message of the text.

It is worth going through the Pastoral Constitution with the following question in mind: In what, for *Gaudium et spes*, does human dignity consist? It is plain that the answer cannot simply be autonomous choice since the document speaks of the need not only to recognise human dignity but to elevate and perfect it (for example in paragraphs 17 and 19). For such perfecting it seeks education of mind and purification of the heart (for instance in paragraph 14). At various points it emphasises the building of moral character through the cultivation of the virtues and the extirpation of the vices. At paragraph 40 it speaks of the Church's 'healing and elevating impact' on the dignity of the person. It does not sell out to the characteristically Modern, whether Liberal or Marxian, position that justice is best established not through the formation of just persons (the view of the ancients from Plato to St Thomas More) but by putting in place the most appropriate structures and procedures in society. This personal justice must surely be in mind when the Constitution says in paragraph 26 that freedom must be founded on truth, built on justice and animated by love: it is hard to see how structures and procedures can be said to *love* – of all things. *Gaudium et spes* stresses that people must exercise their rights in the light of the moral law or they will diminish their dignity. Thus paragraph 41:

> We are tempted to think that our personal rights are fully ensured only when we are exempt from every requirement of divine law.

But this way lies not the maintenance of the dignity of the human person, but its destruction.

Indeed, in paragraph 43 we learn how the 'well-formed Christian conscience' has to see to it that 'the divine law is inscribed in the life of the earthly city'. And more widely, through allusions scattered throughout the body of the text, it is possible to assemble from the Pastoral Constitution the summary of the threefold ground of human dignity later given by John Paul II in *Christifideles laici:* created in God's image and likeness, redeemed by Jesus Christ, destined for eternal life in communion with God.[53]

Conclusion

Gilson, whom I've already quoted, considered that the changeover in the patristic world from pagan to Christian ethics consists precisely in adding such theocentric reference to a description of the life of the virtues.

> They [the Christians] regarded the soul of a just man as beautiful and worthy of honour because virtuous, but virtue itself as honourable only because it leads to God. It is therefore not the supreme good, the *nec plus ultra*, that it was to the Greeks, the all-sufficient unconditioned condition of all morality.[54]

A Gospel of life cannot be just a matter of rational ethics though rational ethics is a good start; it must also be a proclamation of the vocation to divine communion which is open to all who bear the name of human, even in the womb, even when in terminal illness they cannot speak a word.

Clearly, we are not living in felicitous times, either in civil society or – up to a point – in the Church. I began by saying I was about to teach my grandmother to suck eggs, and I end in the same

---

[53] *Christifideles laici* 37. Thus: for created in God's image and likeness, apart from paragraphs 12 and 22, paragraphs 17 and 21; for redeemed by Jesus Christ, paragraphs 13, 22, 37, 38, and 58; for destined for eternal communion with God, paragraphs 13, 19 and 21.

[54] E. Gilson, *The Spirit of Medieval Philosophy*, op. cit., p. 325.

way. What I want to point out by way of conclusion is, such times are fruitful in opportunities to form the virtue of fortitude. In the muck gold can glimmer. J.R.R. Tolkien puts it well in words given to Haldir in *The Lord of the Rings*:

> The world is indeed full of peril, and in it there are many dark places; but still there is much that is fair, and though in all lands love is now mingled with grief, it grows perhaps the greater.[55]

---

[55] J. R. R. Tolkien, *The Lord of the Rings* (London 2005, 50th Anniversary Edition), pp. 348-349.

POPE PIUS XII AND THE GOSPEL OF LIFE

Fr John Saward

Just before four o'clock in the morning, on the ninth of October 1958, Pope Pius XII surrendered his soul to God. He had received the last Sacraments, and Holy Mass *pro infirmo* had been offered in his private chapel. While he was still conscious, he had said the *Anima Christi*, joined in the recitation of the Rosary, and kissed the crucifix several times. After an agony of nine hours, he entered peacefully into eternal life. Cardinal Tisserant, Dean of the Sacred College, made the announcement of his passing: 'We adore the will of the Lord and pray He admit His faithful servant, who on earth represented Jesus, His only-begotten Son, into the company of the holy Pontiffs'. In the days that followed, it seemed as if the whole world was in mourning. As soon as Israel's foreign minister, Golda Meir, received the news, she cabled the Vatican with this message: 'We share in the grief of humanity...When fearful martyrdom came to our people in the decade of Nazi terror, the voice of the Pope was raised for the victims. The life of our times was enriched by a voice speaking out on the great moral truths above the tumult of daily conflict. We mourn a great servant of peace.' A 'servant of peace', indeed: in the inscription he composed for the tomb, the great Latinist Cardinal Bacci (later a supporter of the Ottaviani intervention), calls Pope Pius *Pacis conciliator*. He also gives him the title *Urbis defensor*, for this Roman of the Romans, as the present Holy Father has reminded us, would not leave his beloved City and was ready, had it come to it, to die amidst its ruins. But Bacci could have coined another and equally appropriate name for the Angelic Pastor, *Vitae defensor,* or even *Evangelista vitae*. During the war, Pope Pius saved the lives of many hundreds of thousands of Jewish people, the blood-brethren of God, but throughout his pontificate, with heroic clarity and persistence, he also defended the inviolability of the life of every human being, from fertilisation to natural death, against the assaults of that world turned against

God which his successors have called the 'culture of death'.

In what follows, I intend to do two things: first, I shall give some examples of Pope Pius's preaching of the Gospel of Life; secondly, I shall discuss his teaching on spiritual fatherhood, by which, I shall argue, starting from the Pope's principles, the priest is truly an *evangelista vitae*. All of Papa Pacelli's successors have built upon, and explicitly cited, his teachings on human life. As a phrase and a title, *Evangelium vitae* is proper to Pope John Paul II, but the reality it denotes is what every Pope from the beginning has been called to defend and expound, for the Gospel of Life is really identical with the Gospel of Christ, who is Life in Himself, the Resurrection and the Life. As Pope John Paul says: 'The Gospel of Life lies at the heart of the message of Jesus. Lovingly received day after day by the Church, it is to be preached with dauntless fidelity as "good news" to men of every age and culture.' John Paul preached the Gospel of Life with such fidelity, so, too, did the Pope of Karol Wojtyła's early priesthood, Pius XII, and so, too, must we priests today, in communion with the present Vicar of Christ.

Pope Pius on the Gospel of Life

Reading the Footnotes

This business of the hermeneutic of continuity is not complicated: its first rule is, *Read the footnotes*, something some of the people who call themselves theologians seem reluctant to do. Take the footnotes of Vatican II. They constitute the largest apparatus of any Council in the history of the Church; no Council, except perhaps for Trent, has displayed its continuity with the preceding Tradition in greater documentary detail. Now, if you read the footnotes of Vatican II, you'll find that the individual authority most cited, after the authors of Sacred Scripture, is Pope Pius XII. Time and again, consulting the Pian reference unlocks the conciliar teaching. Now, when we read the footnotes of the conciliar and post-conciliar documents concerned with the precious good of human life and the evils that presently attack it, we find repeated references to the addresses of Pope Pius XII: most notably, in 1951 to the Italian Association of Catholic Midwives; in the same year to the Family Campaign; in 1953 to the Spanish Conference on Genetics; and in 1958 to the Seventh Congress of the International Society of Haematology. All of these documents, as well as the Pian encyclicals, are precious resources of the Tradition and re-pay careful study. As Pope Benedict has said, Pope Pius's teachings 'still possess an extraordinary *attualità* and continue to be a reliable point of reference'.

Anthropology, Epistemology, and Metaphysics

In his moral teaching, Pope Pius sought, as did later Pope John Paul II, to set forth the foundations of that teaching in the philosophy and theology of man; indeed, he would often dig even deeper into epistemology and metaphysics. I suspect that he was the first Pope to deploy the term 'relativism' to describe the intellectual malaise of modernity. His predecessors, from Blessed Pius IX onwards, had condemned the reality of that error, though without the name, frequently and systematically, and Pope Pius builds upon their legacy. At a time when men's minds are in danger of losing their sense of objective truth, first in the intellectual order and then in the moral, Papa Pacelli saw it as indispensably necessary, when speaking to scientists, even if they were good Catholics, to remind them of the human mind's capacity to apprehend reality outside of itself. Thus in his address to the First International Conference on Genetics, delivered less than a month before he died, before considering the moral questions that emerge out of the practice of this relatively new science, Pope Pius reminds his audience that 'truth must be understood as the harmony of man's judgement with the reality of the being and action of things themselves'. Truth is not, and cannot be, he says, 'the harmony of one's personal thinking with the public or scientific opinion of the moment'. Pius refers the geneticists to his encyclical, *Humani generis,* of 1950, in which he had likewise re-affirmed realist metaphysics and epistemology. In all fields, the Pope insists, summarising the encyclical, the human mind must 'maintain intact the great ontological laws, for without them it is impossible to grasp reality'. 'We are thinking', he goes on to say, 'of the principles of contradiction, sufficient reason, of causality, and finality'. The culture of death, in which God's precious infants are slain in the womb and the helpless sick condemned to death by starvation and thirst, is the culture in which those first principles of human reason are flouted, in which it is common, for example, to hear people say, 'You have your truth, I have mine', or 'I don't believe in abortion personally, but I defend the woman's right to choose', and so on. Such is the dictatorship of relativism, the delusion of relativism, the destruction unleashed by relativism. Chesterton prophesied that the Catholic Church would be the last defender of human reason in a world plunged into unreason, and so it has come to be.

As regards the Christian doctrine of man, Pope Pius was responsible for an immensely rich 'theology of the body' anticipating and in some ways even surpassing in its detailed applications the teaching known by that name of his successor, John Paul II. Speaking as he often did to groups of medical specialists, Pius discussed at length the goodness and beauty of the various organs and functions of the human body: the ear, the nose, and the throat, the eye, the mouth, the gums. These medical addresses are a practical demonstration of the harmony between faith and reason, the true religion and true science, and a triumphant affirmation, against all Manichaeism, of the principle, *caro cardo salutis*, 'The flesh is the hinge of salvation'. The fundamental principles underlying them all are that man has been created by God as a unity of soul and body, that it is therefore, Pope Pius says, 'from the Creator that [man] has the right to his body and his life', and that he is redeemed in both body and soul by the Father's eternal Word incarnate.

The proper title of Pope John Paul II's General Audience Addresses on 'The Theology of the Body' is 'The Redemption of the Body and the sacramentality of Marriage'. Following the Fathers and Doctors, Papa Wojtyla insists that in the resurrection men will be raised as men, and women as women, with the sexual identity of their human bodies, their nuptial meaning, preserved and glorified forever. Now Pope Pius XII, in defining the dogma of our Lady's bodily Assumption, anticipated this important part of his successor's theology of the body. Consider, for example, this argument that he takes from the Seraphic Doctor, St Bonaventure: 'Her blessedness would not have been complete unless she were there as a person. The soul is not a person, but the soul, joined to the body, is a person. It is manifest that she is there in soul and in body. Otherwise she would not possess her complete beatitude.' Again, he quotes another Franciscan, St Bernardine of Siena, who argues that 'it is reasonable and fitting that not only the soul and body of a man, but also the soul and body of a woman should have obtained heavenly glory'. If men are not raised as men, nor women as women, St Bernardine's argument would not hold, but because by the will and work of God there are two different and complementary sexes, in the state of glory as well as in the condition of mortality, it follows that it is indeed most fitting that a woman, the New Eve, should already share as a complete person in the Resurrection of her Son, and alongside Him, the God-Man, the New Adam. Towards the end of the Apostolic Constitution, Pope Pius further unfolds this moral and anthropological aspect of the dogma of the Assumption:

> It is to be hoped [he says] that, while materialism and the corruption of morals, its natural consequence, threaten to swamp virtue and to destroy human life by bringing on wars, the noble destiny of souls and bodies may be made blindingly apparent. It is to be hoped, finally, that faith in the bodily Assumption of Mary into Heaven may render more firm and more active our faith in our own resurrection.

Contraception: Closure against Life

The most widespread of all the moral evils directed against the gift of life is contraception: as the name suggests, *contraception*, is against something, opposed to something, blocks something, practically speaking is hostile to something; contraception is contra-life, contra-child. In his preaching of the Gospel of Life, Pope Pius, at great length and on many occasions, reminded the faithful, and indeed all mankind, that marriage, by the will of the Creator, has as its 'primary and intimate end' the procreation and education of a new life, and that therefore, in any use of marriage, to frustrate the conjugal act of its capacity to procreate is gravely sinful. To avoid any doubt, on 30th March 1944, Pope Pius approved a declaration of the Holy Office on the order of the ends of marriage, in which, as he put it later in a speech to newlyweds, the Sacred Congregation re-affirms 'what has been handed down by Christian tradition, what the Supreme Pontiffs have repeatedly taught, and what was afterwards formulated in the Code of Canon Law'.

Now, on this question of the ends of marriage, we have a test for the hermeneutic of continuity. Haven't so many of the seminary professors conveyed the impression that the Church at the Council quietly dropped, even disowned, the doctrine of the ordered ends of marriage? With such an interpretation of the Tradition, the Benedictine hermeneutic of continuity requires us to disagree. If the Church is one consistent person through the ages, how can she abandon in the 1960s what in the 1950s she had stated so vigorously, through the Vicar of her Spouse, to be the teaching of the whole Christian tradition and all the Supreme Pontiffs? To practise the hermeneutic of continuity in this matter, we must make a distinction: *in words* the doctrine may not be so evident, but *in concept* the doctrine re-stated by Pope Pius remains present and presupposed.

In *Gaudium et spes*, the Council Fathers state that 'marriage and married love are by nature ordered to the procreation and education of children; indeed, children are the supreme gift of marriage and greatly contribute to the good of the parents themselves' (n. 50). Now the good to which nature orders something is its primary end or purpose: for example, the good to which nature orders the lungs is breathing. Therefore, the Council's teaching has essentially the same meaning as Pope Pius's: the primary end to which the sexual union of husband and wife is ordered by nature is procreation. Moreover, if married *love* is ordered to procreation, then again it follows that the good of procreation must be primary within marriage. The kind of love that unites man and woman in marriage is a love that takes them out of themselves towards another person, 'the third person', the child. As Pope John Paul said in one of his General Audience addresses: 'Procreation brings it about that "the man and the woman" (his wife) know each other reciprocally in "the third" originated by both'. This suggests an end, a fulfilment, towards which their married love points, even when it does not attain it.

I said a moment ago that, to practise the hermeneutic of continuity, we have to read the footnotes. Another indispensable principle is: *Check the conciliar Acta*. Now on this question the *Acta* of Vatican II inform us that, when the draft of *Gaudium et spes* was being discussed, one hundred and ninety Fathers of the Council asked for it to include an explicit reference to the 'hierarchical connection' of the ends of marriage. The Conciliar Commission replied as follows:

> [I]n a text that addresses the world in a direct and pastoral style, it is obvious that highly technical terms such as 'hierarchy' should be avoided. In any case, [the Commission goes on to say] the primordial aspect (*momentum primordiale*) of procreation and education is expounded at least ten times in the text (*Acta synodalia*, vol. 4, pars 7, 478).

This exchange confirms the argument presented already, namely, that the text of *Gaudium et spes* expresses the doctrine of procreation as the primary end of marriage in equivalent terms. Pope Pius himself finds another, more 'direct and pastoral' way of re-stating the doctrine when he says, in his Address to the Associations of Large Families, that 'marriage is an institution at the service of life'.

When Pope Paul in *Humanae Vitae* speaks of the inseparability within each individual conjugal act of 'the significance of unity' and 'the significance of procreation', he is likewise not denying that procreation is the primary end or purpose of marriage and the conjugal act, he is simply placing them within a genus other than 'end' in order the more effectively to show their inseparability. Dietrich von Hildebrand prepared for this approach when he argued that procreation was the primary end of marriage, while love was its *meaning*. Wedded love, he says, is what 'ennobles sex', which seems to be saying that, if procreation is the final cause of marriage, married love is its formal cause.

Pope John Paul stays within the category of meaning or signification when he says, in his General Audience Addresses on the Theology of the Body, that the 'language' which the body speaks in the sexual union of husband and wife, the 'meaning' conveyed by the conjugal act, is twofold, love and potential fruitfulness, and that artificially to separate these two meanings, to deprive the conjugal act of its procreative capacity, frustrates its capacity for loving union. To contracept is to contradict what the bodies of husband and wife are saying by their union; it deprives the conjugal act of its grounding in truth and thus of the grandeur of its love.

Whether we speak of ends or meanings or causes, what all the Popes, from Pius XII to Benedict XVI, want us to do is to remember the inseparability, in every act of sexual intercourse, of loving union and procreation. The uniting of man and woman in love through the conjugal act, says Pope Pius, is willed by the Creator, for man and woman serve God in the transmission of life precisely as rational creatures, created in God's image, endowed with mind and heart, and therefore with the capacity to make a conscious and free gift of themselves in love.

> The marital act [says Pope Pius, speaking to the Italian midwives], in its natural setting, is a personal action. It is the simultaneous and direct co-operation of husband and wife, which, by the very nature of the agents and the propriety of the act, is the expression of the mutual giving, which, in the words of Scripture, results in the union 'in one flesh'.

Thus, with complete consistency, the Church, through Pope Pius, condemned as gravely sinful not only contraception and direct sterilisation, by which the act of conjugal love is intentionally closed against life, but also artificial insemination, the attempt to procreate life without the act of conjugal love. In responding to the technology of 'assisted reproduction' of more recent years, the Church has added arguments to those of Pope Pius, but the primary consideration remains the same: the good of procreation must be attained by the 'personal action' of the spouses in conjugal intercourse.

One final thought, which I borrow from Monsignor Cormac Burke. To speak of something being ordered to something else is not to disparage it, but to 'give the key to its true nature'.

And so the Church, in teaching that mutual love in marriage is subordinated to procreation, far from slighting human love, is giving us the key to nature's plan for the fulfilment, within marriage, of the great expectations of human love.

Abortion

In his Address to Italian Midwives, delivered in 1951, Pope Pius re-affirmed with the utmost clarity the inviolability of human life from the first moment of fertilisation to the last moment of natural death:

[E]very human being, even a child in his mother's womb, has the right to life directly from God, and not from his parents, from any human society or authority. Therefore, there is no man, no human authority, no science, no 'indication' whatsoever, medical, eugenic, social, economic, moral, that may lend a valid juridical right for the deliberate direct disposal of an innocent human life, that is, a disposal aiming at its destruction, either as an objective or as a means to another objective in no way, perhaps, illicit in itself. Thus, for example, to save a mother's life is a very noble aim. But the direct killing of the child as a means to that end is not licit.

In the same year, speaking to the Family Campaign, Pope Pius responds to the calumny often directed against Catholic teaching, namely, that the child's life must be 'preferred' to that of the mother.

Never and in no case [says the Pope] has the Church taught that the child's life must be preferred to that of the mother. It is a mistake to formulate the question with this alternative: either the child's life or the mother's. No: neither the mother's life not the child's may be submitted to an act of direct suppression. For the one and for the other, the requirement can be only this: to make every effort to save the life of both the mother and the child.

Now, of course, there are cases where, as the Pope says, 'the mother's death must be reckoned with'. In such circumstances, according to the principle of double effect, as Pius explains (without using the phrase), a procedure to save the mother's life would be licit, even though the death of her child would be a consequence, albeit unintended and indirect, of the procedure. However, Pope Pius mentions the possibility of a mother bravely insisting on carrying her baby to birth despite the danger to herself. Nine years later an Italian mother and physician, Gianna Beretta Molla, would make such a decision, and, for her heroic faith, courage, and love for God and her child, has now been raised to the honours of the altar. She was diagnosed during pregnancy with a uterine tumour. Instead of permitting the surgeons to perform a morally licit procedure that would have indirectly caused the death of her child, she asked the surgeon simply to remove the tumour. Then, at the birth of the child, she asked the doctors, if in an ensuing crisis they felt forced to choose, to concentrate their efforts on saving the life of her child. Seven days later, she died of septic peritonitis, praying, 'Jesus, I love you!' The heavenly glory of St Gianna, whose adult life coincided exactly with the pontificate of Pius XII, and the earthly life of her child, are two of the greatest fruits of Pope Pius's proclamation of the Gospel of Life.

Euthanasia

In the Address to Midwives, as in the Address to the Family Front, Pope Pius condemns all direct attacks on human life, not only at its beginning through abortion, but also towards its end through euthanasia. What is more, in both addresses, he compares the theory and practice of euthanasia by doctors in the post-war world with the euthanasia programme of the National Socialists in Germany.

The direct destruction of so-called 'worthless lives', before or after birth, practised in great numbers a few years ago, cannot in any way be justified. Consequently, when that practice began, the Church expressly declared it to be contrary to natural, divine, and positive law, and therefore illicit to kill – even by order of a public authority – those who, though innocent, are nevertheless, on account of a physical or psychological deficiency, not useful to people, but will rather become a burden to it. The life of an innocent creature is inviolable, and any direct attempt or aggression against it is a violation of one of the fundamental laws without which safe social living is not possible.

One of the reasons why euthanasia is gravely morally evil, according to Pope Pius, is that it deprives the suffering person of the opportunity to offer up his sufferings in union with Christ for the glory of God and the salvation of mankind; it deprives him of participation in that apostolate of suffering of which St Paul spoke when he said that in his own flesh he made up what is lacking in Christ's afflictions for the good of the Church, Christ's Mystical Body (cf *Col* 1:24).

Pope Pius on the Priest as the Servant of the Gospel of Life: The Priest as Father in Christ

Spiritual fatherhood is one of the most striking themes in the teaching of Pope Pius on the priesthood. For example, in his discourse to the parish priests and Lenten preachers of Rome in 1940, he says that the mission of the parish priest can be summed up in three titles: apostle, father, shepherd. Speaking to newlyweds the following year, he sets priestly paternity in the grand context of the Incarnation and its purpose of redemption, and shows the likenesses and unlikenesses of the two paternities, physical and spiritual:

> When the Son of God deigned to become man, the word of the Saviour of the human race restored to its primal splendour the marriage bond of man and wife which human passions had degraded from its noble founding. He elevated it to a great

sacrament by His union with His Bride, the Church, our Mother, made fruitful by His divine Blood, in which we are re-born through the word of faith and the saving waters. And to those who believe in His name, it gives the power of becoming the children of God, 'who were born not of blood nor of the will of the flesh, nor of the will of man, but of God' (*Jn* 1:13). In these solemn words of the Gospel of St John we recognise a double paternity: the paternity of flesh through the will of man, and the paternity of God through the power of spirit and divine grace; two paternities that, among Christian people, create and seal through the priesthood and through marriage the fathers of the spirit and supernatural life, and the fathers of the flesh and natural life; two Sacraments instituted by Christ for His Church to guarantee and perpetuate through the centuries the generation and re-generation of the children of God. Two Sacraments, two paternities, two fathers – partners who complement each other in the education of offspring, the gift of God, the hope of the family, of the Church, of earth and of Heaven.

The ordained man, like the married man, has the task of begetting life, spiritual and supernatural life in the case of the priest, bodily and natural life in the case of the father of the family. However, while the two fatherhoods are essentially distinct, they are united in theory by analogy, and in practice by their co-operation in the education of children. A married man's conceiving of the child in the womb of his wife is but the physical beginning of his fatherhood; while he still draws breath, he has to work with his wife in the moral and spiritual formation of the child, and what he does at home is inseparable from what the priest does for the child by the Sacraments and his teaching. Pope Pius quotes what he calls the 'clear doctrine' of St Thomas, who says that the Sacrament of Matrimony makes parents 'the propagators and preservers of spiritual life in accordance with a ministry which is at the same time physical and spiritual', which consists in 'generating offspring and educating them in divine worship'. Therefore, Pope Pius concludes, speaking directly to newlyweds, 'always under the guidance of the priest, you are the first and closest educators and teachers of the children given and entrusted to you by God'.

This beautiful teaching of Pope Pius inspires several thoughts in me. First, in this Year of St Paul, it opens up a fresh perspective on the Apostle of the Gentiles. In the epistle to the Ephesians, he teaches us that all fatherhood, physical and spiritual, in Heaven and on earth is 'named' from the Father of our Lord Jesus Christ (cf *Ep* 3:14f), that is, in some way imitates it and participates in it. St Paul himself exemplifies spiritual fatherhood in his apostolic and priestly office. The Apostle, who for the love of Christ and for the sake of a greater availability to Him has renounced the good of marriage and with it the possibility of physical fatherhood, tells us that he became a 'father in Christ Jesus' to the Corinthians 'through the Gospel' (1 *Co* 4:15), that is, through the preaching of the Gospel and the administering of the Sacraments of the Gospel. (St Augustine likewise says that St Ambrose became a father to him by baptising him.) Now one expression of St Paul's fatherhood in Christ Jesus is his teaching on the morality of Christian marriage, for example, on its essential unity and the obligation of husbands and wives to render the debt (cf 1 *Co* 7:2ff).

The example of the Apostle suggests a general principle of priestly fatherhood. While as an ordained instrument of the Eternal High Priest, the priest is directly at the service of supernatural life, he is also, indirectly, and especially by his teaching on marriage and the family, at the service of natural life. Precisely as a father in Christ, and an icon of Christ the Bridegroom, the priest has the duty to teach his people, as the Apostle did, about the nature, essential properties, and proper goods of marriage. Our failure to guide husbands and wives in their service of life, whether in marriage preparation, or in the confessional, or in the pulpit, is a failure in our own spiritual fatherhood.

Secondly, the Pope's witness to the priest's spiritual fatherhood in God reminds us of the absolute necessity, by the will of Christ and therefore the unchangeable doctrine and law of His Church, of the maleness of the ordained man. Since the supernatural presupposes the natural, it follows that the supernatural fatherhood of Word and Sacrament can only be received and exercised by one who is a member of the sex called by God to natural fatherhood. God's gift of Holy Order in the Church presupposes, and bears witness to, His prior gift of sexual order to mankind. In the case of the Anglicans, a line of logical inevitability connects their official approval of contraception at the Lambeth conference of 1928 with their decision in 1992 to ordain women and the determination of so many of them today to recognise as morally licit conduct that not only the Fathers and Doctors of the Church but the original founders of their denomination regarded as a sin crying to Heaven for vengeance. At every stage, in each new departure from universal Christian tradition, the trend is *contra naturam*. We could take the diagnosis of the disease further back in history, to even deeper causes: the loss of devotion to our blessed Lady and of a sense of the Church as Virgin, Mother, and Bride; Henry VIII's destruction of monasticism, and his assault on Christian marriage and the jurisdiction over marriage of the Church built on Peter; the flight from the sacramental principle and its establishment by the Incarnation, a flight, then, from the flesh, the hinge of salvation.

Thirdly, the priest exercises his spiritual fatherhood, and therefore his service of the Gospel of Life, through the offering of the Holy Sacrifice of the Mass and the administering of the other Sacraments. As Pope Pius says:

> By the design of God, the priest, like the bishop, 'taken from among men, is appointed for men in the things that pertain to God, that he may offer up gifts and sacrifices for sins' (*Heb* 5:1). That is the reason why the sacred character of the priest, as the intermediary between God and men, is revealed, manifested, and unfolded in all its dignity and at its most sublime, within the radiance of the sovereign light of his ministry, in the Holy Sacrifice of the Mass and in the administration of the Sacraments.

The Pope goes on to speak beautifully about how through the Sacraments, as an 'instrument of the power and love and pardon and redemption that has been bestowed on fallen man', the priest enables his fellow man to 'free himself from slavery and escape from the snares of Satan, so that he can return to his heavenly Father, as a pilgrim re-born, clothed in grace, heir to Heaven, refreshed and strengthened for the journey by a heavenly bread which is more living and wholesome than the fruit of the tree of life planted in the earthly paradise'. Thus, through the seven rivers of divine grace flowing from the Trinitarian Godhead through the pierced Heart of the Son, the priest serves life, supernatural life, eternal life, man's transfiguration by participation in God's own life.

Now is there any way in which, through the Sacraments, the priest serves the protection of *natural* human life? Most certainly: three examples come to mind. The first is the Sacrament of Matrimony, in which, though the priest is not, on the traditional understanding, the minister of the Sacrament, he is nevertheless deputed by God and the Church to bless the marriage. Now prominent among the blessings from God for which he prays is the good of offspring, and indeed the good, for the couple, of a long life on earth: 'May you see your children's children to the third and fourth generation, and may you live to a ripe old age.'

The second way in which priest proclaims the Gospel of Life through the administering of the Sacraments is through his ministry to the sick and dying. In a culture of death, in which euthanasia and assisted suicide are being promoted with increasing vehemence, we must make renewed acts of faith in the objective efficacy of the Sacraments that we confer at the end of life. Christ, the divine Physician, Christ who is the Life and the Resurrection, through the priest, His living image and instrument, and through the holy oil, brings peace to the troubled souls of the sick and confers on them the grace to make their final agony the last and greatest act of their pilgrimage of faith, a dying 'to the Lord', as St Paul says, a dying for the love of Him, and, in silence and hiddenness, for the good of the whole Mystical Body of Christ.

Thirdly, and most importantly, in offering the Holy Sacrifice of the Mass, in which the Sacrifice of the Cross is re-presented and its saving power poured out afresh, the priest can and ought to pray for the conversion of hearts and minds to gratitude and reverence for

God's precious gift of life. The Fathers of the Council of Trent, in defining the propitiatory effect of the the Eucharistic Sacrifice, says that 'the Lord, appeased by this oblation, grants grace and the gift of repentance'. The masters of sacred doctrine explain that the atoning force of the Precious Blood, through the Mass, can and does confer the actual graces that move a person to turn away from sin and come back to God. If this is so, should we not, Fathers, from time to time, offer the Holy Sacrifice for the conversion of those caught up in the violence and depravity of the abortion industry? In proclaiming Christ's Death at the altar, we proclaim His Gospel of Life.

Finally, before leaving this theme of the priest's fatherly service of life, let me say that, of course, a priest is a son before he is a father. *Pro patribus tuis nati sunt tibi filii,* as the Psalmist says, 'In place of thy fathers sons are born to thee' (*Ps* 44:17), a text St Augustine interprets to mean that only those who are first by Baptism and faith the sons of the Church may serve her as fathers, bishops in succession to the Apostles. 'Such is the Catholic Church', he says, 'she has given birth to sons who, through all the earth, continue the work of her first Fathers'. Now the Church's Mother, her supreme model, pre-eminent member, and living embodiment, is our blessed Lady, given by the Crucified to all Christians, but especially to priests, in the person of John. We can, therefore, develop St Augustine's teaching and say: 'Only those who are devoted sons of Mary can be effective fathers in Christ.' Pope Pius, in his 1950 Apostolic Exhortation *Menti nostrae,* says that devotion to the Virgin Mother of Priests is an indispensable means of priestly sanctification: 'Although the burning love of the Virgin Mother of God embraces all, she loves in a special manner priests, who reproduce in themselves the living image of Jesus Christ.' That love in our Blessed Mother's Heart has one goal in our regard: the perfecting of our configuration to her Son, in the acts of our ministry and in the virtues of our lives. The Blessed Virgin gave life to Him who is Life, and, now glorified even bodily in eternal life, she will by her motherly protection, if we let her, keep us faithful to the preaching of Christ's Gospel of Life, of the Christ who is the Gospel of Life in His very person.

Conclusion: Thy Kingdom Come!

There is no way to overcome the culture of death, no other path to the civilisation of love, than, by Mary's prayers, to help our fellow human beings to know and love the Lord Jesus Christ, true God and true man, in His one true Church, the Catholic Church. Only where He is acknowledged as King can there be a 'reign of truth and life, of sanctity and grace, of justice, love, and peace'. This was the message of Pope Pius XI in *Quas primas*, as it was also of his co-operator and successor, Pius XII. In the opening words of his first encyclical, Papa Pacelli recalled Pope Leo XIII's consecration of mankind, forty years earlier, to the Sacred Heart of Jesus, and then made a pledge:

> We, as a newly ordained priest, then just empowered to recite, 'I will go unto to the altar of God', hailed [Pope Leo's] Encyclical *Annum Sacrum* with approval, enthusiasm, and delight as a message from Heaven. We associated Ourselves in fervent admiration with the motives and aims that inspired and directed the truly providential action of a Pontiff so sure in his diagnosis of the open and hidden needs and sores of his day. It is only natural, then, that We should today feel profoundly grateful to Providence for having designed that the first year of Our Pontificate should be associated with a memory so precious and so dear of Our first year of priesthood, and that We should take the opportunity of paying homage to the King of kings and Lord of Lords as a kind of Introit prayer to Our Pontificate, in the spirit of Our renowned predecessor and in the faithful accomplishment of his designs, and that, in fine, We should make of it the Alpha and Omega of Our aims, of Our hopes, of Our teaching, of Our activity, of Our patience and of Our sufferings, by consecrating them all to the spread of the Kingdom of Christ. [He then goes on to say:] At the head of the road which leads to the spiritual and moral bankruptcy of the present day stand the nefarious efforts of not a few to dethrone Christ; the abandonment of the law of truth which He proclaimed, and of the law of love which

is the life breath of His Kingdom. In the recognition of the royal prerogatives of Christ and in the return of individuals and of society to the law of His truth and of His love lies the only way to salvation.

There is no other way: the God-Man, Jesus Christ, is the Way, as He is the Life. Men will not fully respect His gift of natural life, as they cannot securely attain His gift of eternal life, without following Him within the Catholic unity of His Mystical Body. Yes, in our pro-life efforts, we can and must reach out to men of good will, and to those of the separated brethren, a sadly small number, ready to work with us in the defence of human life. We are Catholics, and therefore respect reason, for faith and reason are together, as Pope John Paul says so beautifully, the wings by which the human mind flies up to the truth. The strength of our understanding of natural law, of the capacity of human reason to apprehend reality outside itself, including the great religious and moral truths, is that it enables us to engage in coherent dialogue and argument with men not blessed with the gift of faith. Yes, *but* we also believe, as of faith, that human nature bears wounds consequent upon the sin of Adam, weakened intellects and wills, disordered passions, vulnerability to the influences of a world hostile to Christ, and to tempting by the fallen angel who is the usurping prince of that world. We believe, too, that, though not every action of a man without faith and the grace of Christ is a sin, no man can fulfil the entire moral law, and avoid grave temptation, without what the Council of Trent calls the 'special help of God'. Only when men assent fully to the truth of Christ as taught by His Church, and allow themselves to be transformed by His grace through the Sacraments of the Church, only when Christ the King reigns in the hearts and societies of men, can life triumph over death. That conviction is the beginning and the end of Pope Pius XII's preaching of the Gospel of Life. May it be ours, too. *Lord Jesus, thy Kingdom, come.*

CHALLENGES AND OPPORTUNITIES IN PRO-LIFE PREACHING

Fr Timothy Finigan

A word about preaching
The Gospel of the Day

I must first address briefly a worry or scruple that some priests may have. Should we not be guided in our preaching by the scripture provided for us? Is that not the Word the Holy Spirit is guiding us to break for the people?

Many priests have already resolved this question in the face of widespread ignorance of the basics of the Catholic faith. A minority of our people will attend courses for adult education in the parishes. The Sunday homily is the major opportunity that we have to help people to grow in their knowledge and love of the faith. We can do so in the light of the scriptures, either by lectionary-based catechesis or by a Catechism-based programme which feeds on the Word of God as it is given to us week by week. I do not intend to spend time discussing these approaches although I think they are perfectly valid. I believe that there is an additional and reason for us to be diligent in pro-life preaching.[56]

Preaching and Life

Preaching is not intended to be esoteric and divorced from the daily lives of the people to whom we are preaching. As *Gaudium et Spes* put it:

> The Gospel of Christ constantly renews the life and culture of fallen man, it combats and removes the errors and evils resulting from the permanent allurement of sin. It never eases to purify and elevate the morality of peoples. By riches coming from above,

---

[56] Cf. also Fr Frank Pavone, *A Note On Liturgical Norms For Homilies* online at www.priestsforlife.org/preaching/litnorms.html (Accessed 21/11/06).

it makes fruitful, as it were from within, the spiritual qualities and traditions of every people and of every age. It strengthens, perfects and restores them in Christ. Thus the Church, in the very fulfillment of her own function, stimulates and advances human and civic culture; by her action, also by her liturgy, she leads them toward interior liberty.[57]

With regard to the liturgical homily, the General Instruction of the Roman Missal says that the homily should "take into account both the mystery being celebrated and the particular needs of the listeners."[58]

Pope John Paul referred particularly to the place of the Gospel of Life in our preaching:

> The Gospel of Life is at the heart of Jesus' message. Lovingly received day after day by the Church, it is to be preached with dauntless fidelity as "good news" to the people of every age and culture.[59]

Duty of pro-life preaching

If we consider the particular needs of our people in the United Kingdom today, we must be aware that one of the most pressing needs of our listeners is to hear the "good news" of the Gospel of Life that Pope John Paul placed at the heart of the message of Our Lord. The challenges and opportunities that I will outline impose a duty on us to preach on these matters regularly and as effectively as we can. We could make our own in this particular respect the exclamation of St Paul "Woe to me if I do not preach the Gospel" (1 *Co* 9:16)

Challenges to preaching the Gospel of Life

I will consider two areas which present challenges for pro-life preaching. I will be brief since I have no desire to engage in a

---
[57] *Gaudium et Spes* n.58.
[58] General Instruction of the Roman Missal (2005) n.65.
[59] Pope John Paul II *Evangelium Vitae* (1995) n.1.

lamentation which would waste our valuable time. I will spend more time on our responses to these challenges and the opportunities which I believe are present to us today.

I am specifically considering challenges to our preaching, that is, factors which make it more difficult for us to preach the Gospel of Life effectively so that people hear and their lives are changed. I will consider two challenges related to education and two related to our culture. (I do not claim that they are an exhaustive list.)

Sex-education in schools

I believe that in terms of education in society, the heart of the battle is over the question of sex-education in schools. Those who favour abortion, euthanasia, the homosexual lifestyle, experimentation on human embryos, the widespread provision of contraception, and an amoral attitude to sexual behaviour in general, rightly focus on sex-education in schools as a means of changing hearts and minds.

Sex-education, as it is currently provided, assaults the modesty of children, encouraging them first of all to talk about matters that were, relatively recently, considered too filthy for decent-minded adults to talk about. Sadly, two recent cases highlighted by SPUC show that this is not necessarily absent from Catholic schools.[60] At one school, the "nurse" demonstrated to teenagers how to put a condom onto a plastic model of a penis. She also gave cards indicating where the young people could obtain the *Morning After Pill*. In another, the Channel 4 *Living and Growing* series was used, despite vociferous complaints from parents. The series shows graphic animated cartoons depicting sexual intercourse and the pleasure of masturbation.

Another case came to my attention only last weekend. A Catholic secondary school encouraged children in Year 8 (aged 12-13) to fill in a questionnaire which included asking them about the effectiveness of various methods of contraception in preventing HIV infection and other STIs. One option listed was "sex without penetration."

---

[60] SPUC's Pro Life Times has recently featured stories concerning sex-education at St John's Catholic Comprehensive School in Gravesend and St William of York Junior School in Forest Hill.

Such "education" encourages children to talk openly about the details of sexual activity, destroys any natural reticence about these matters that they may have learned in their home, and helps to promote the standard views of our culture that sexual activity among those under 16 is normal, if not inevitable, and that contraception and abortion are part of the package that goes with this lifestyle.

Outdated attitudes among Catholic clergy

In 1968, *Humanae Vitae* referred principally to the use of birth control within marriage. Moral theologians in the 1960s who wished to change the teaching of the Church spoke generally of married couples. Pope Paul VI clearly prophesied the consequences of failing to maintain the teaching of the Church:

> Responsible men can become more deeply convinced of the truth of the doctrine laid down by the Church on this issue if they reflect on the consequences of methods and plans for artificial birth control. Let them first consider how easily this course of action could open wide the way for marital infidelity and a general lowering of moral standards. Not much experience is needed to be fully aware of human weakness and to understand that human beings – and especially the young, who are so exposed to temptation – need incentives to keep the moral law, and it is an evil thing to make it easy for them to break that law.[61]

Had an orthodox moral theologian suggested in 1968 that the consequences would include civil partnerships for homosexual people, demonstration of the use of condoms for children, secret abortions for girls under 16, *In Vitro* Fertilisation and the discarding of "spare" embryos, they would have been dismissed as alarmist and unrealistic.

However, it is not uncommon for clergy discussing the question of birth control to speak as though the subject concerned only married couples. Concern over the burden of large families still

---

[61] Paul VI *Humanae Vitae* (1968) n.17.

occupies much of the discussion. Many clergy are unaware of the sheer obscenity of much of the material that is now presented to children. Despite the graphic descriptions in soap operas and reality TV, and plot lines involvin of sexual activity, there are not lacking clergy who are still be duped by the idea that sex education is a necessity to prevent children from growing up ignorant about the facts of life.

There is also considerable ignorance about the impact of what might generically be termed new ecclesial movements. Whether traditional or happy-clappy, the common features of successful work among the young are a strong prayer life focussed on the Blessed Eucharist and Our Lady, a loyal adherence to the teaching of the Church's Magisterium, and, most notably for our purposes, a determined rejection of the moral decay of our culture and a genuine attempt to live decently. Many clergy still labour under the impression that in order to attract the young to the Church, it is necessary to downplay the Church's moral teaching. Nothing could be further from the truth.

Challenges in our culture
Misinformation by the media

Perhaps our most effective enemy in preaching the Gospel of Life is the pervasive propaganda of the culture of death in all of the popular outlets of the traditional mass media.

Every level of society is influenced. At one level, there is the continuing availability of soft pornography in tabloid newspapers and "Lad Mags". At a different level, there is the constant biased coverage of every issue related to the Gospel of Life in the BBC and other mainstream media companies. Every day, every life-related issue that is covered, is subjected to subtle or not so subtle bias in the use of language, the selection of interviewees, the approach to history and literature, and, of course, the picture painted of the Catholic Church.

It has reached a point where I can work out fairly accurately what the BBC has said on any given topic by listening to remarks from parishioners. It is very clear to me that their attitudes and opinions are commonly shaped by what they have seen or heard via the traditional media.

This particular challenge makes our preaching all the more important as it may be the only source of truthful information for our people on many issues, let alone the only source of sound moral teaching.

Personal acquaintance with moral transgressions

From the point of view of pro-life preaching, some priests find it worrying that there might be someone in the congregation who have had an abortion. This is really a part of the "outdated attitudes among the clergy" of which I spoke earlier. We should be in no doubt that it would be very unlikely in a medium sized parish if there were not several women in the congregation who have at one time had an abortion.

The presence of women who have had an abortion is not a reason for not preaching about pro-life issues. On the contrary, it is a compelling reason why we should preach on these matters. The same applies to the many Catholics who have undergone IVF treatment, or who may be living a homosexual lifestyle, and, of course, the countless numbers who regularly use artificial contraception.

In all these cases, if we do not preach the Gospel of Life, all that the people will be left with is the latest caricature of Catholic teaching that they heard on the television or read in a magazine.

Of course, the fact of there being people in the congregation who are directly concerned with these issues does shape to a degree the manner in which we speak. However, if we fear to speak on these issues at all, we should bear in mind the legitimate question that will be asked increasingly by Catholics who discover the beauty of the Church's teaching: "Why did nobody ever tell us?"

Responses: education

Parents and schools

Traditionally, clergy have influenced schools by being a member of the Governing Body. This may still be a way in which to influence a good school. However, clergy often find that their influence is limited by the constraints that are imposed on schools by the Government. In addition, Catholic schools employ significant numbers of non-Catholic staff, and staff who are not practising Catholics. The direct "political" influence of clergy is reducing.

At the same time, parents are becoming more aware of the problems with sex-education in schools. Those who are active in the pro-life movement are often dismayed that the issues on which they are battling in the secular arena also surface in the Catholic school to which they have sent their children. At the simplest level, the fact that their parish priest agrees with them and supports them can be a great consolation. A well constructed letter from a priest to the Headteacher or the Chair of Governors can also have a certain impact.

However, I believe that the most important area of influence for clergy is with the family. To borrow a phrase used in other circles, we need to engage in "consciousness raising." Few parents would consider it acceptable for their primary school age child to be shown an animated cartoon illustrating the joys of masturbation. They need to know that this is being done and they need to be assisted in their efforts to complain.

Education of the clergy

The education of the clergy with regard to the facts of life in today's world is necessary if we are to preach the Gospel of Life effectively. Clergy need to know at least in general terms the enormous increase of STIs during the last ten years: the outcome of contraceptive "sex-education."

These statistics from the Health Protection Agency[62] make depressing reading. The percentage change from 1995-2004 shows large increases in syphillis (1449%), gonorrhea (111%), chlamydia (223%), herpes (15%) and genital warts (32%). The 2003 report to the select committee on Health summarised it well by saying that: The last decade has witnessed a dramatic rise in diagnoses of all

---

[62] Online at www.hpa.org.uk/infections/topics_az/hiv_and_sti/epidemiology/sti_data_1995-2004_Final.pdf (Accessed 21/11/06).

major [sexually transmitted] diseases.[63]

The Office of National Statistics compiled a report showing data on the use of condoms in the previous four weeks. It found that 46% of males and 37% of females with one or more new partners used condoms on every occasion that they had sex. The fact is that the promotion of condoms simply is not achieving a reduction in STIs. On the contrary, there is a massive increase – a greater increase in fact, in those infections that are purportedly protected against by condoms.

Clergy need to know the misery that is caused to so many women by an ill-considered decision to have an abortion at a young age; a decision that continues to haunt them. They need to know some of statistics related to the homosexual lifestyle so that they are better informed when speaking to people about this matter and more strongly motivated to help young people to avoid being drawn into this subculture.

Responses: culture
Innoculation of the laity against the media

When considering the impact of the mass media, it is helpful to understand some of the analysis that has been made of the way that people are influenced by the media.

In the 1970s, Jerry Mander spoke of the apathetic hypnosis into which people fall under the influence of the soap opera or the film. While we can see some truth in this, more recent studies have tended to take a more optimistic view of people's interaction with the media. Thompson[64] found that people's interactions with the media were a part of the general complex of interactions such as telephone conversations and personal contact. We see this, for example, when we are asked "Did you see…?" or when people discuss a television programme.

This is a hopeful point for us. The impact of the mass media is

---

[63] Online at www.publications.parliament.uk/pa/cm200203/cmselect/cmhealth/69/6906.htm (Accessed 21/11/06).

[64] Thompson, J. *The Media and Modernity* (1995).

mediated by other personal interactions. If we are able to show clear instances of bias in the media and explain them, we "break the spell" and our people begin to look at the television in a new way. We need to destroy the trust that people have in the false message given by the mainstream media on pro-life (and other) issues.

Another factor to be considered is the agenda-setting power of the media. One means of undermining this is to persuade people to watch less television and read good publications instead of secular newspapers. Fortunately, it does seem that the all-encompassing empire of the television is beginning to lose its grip on the population and there are significant sectors who are watching television less: notably the young.

Use of new media

Secular commentators have already noticed the most powerful force that is undermining the agenda-setting power of the traditional media: the new media on the internet in the form of blogs, forums, wikis, YouTube and other recent developments. This is very good news for us as I shall explain when I consider the opportunities that are open to us today.

Pastoral compassion

In relation to the question of our parishioners' personal experience of abortion, IVF or homosexuality, we need to reclaim the initiative. Our struggle to overcome the influence of the media is a part of this. But perhaps the most effective means is our own compassionate pastoral work.

A hurdle that we need to overcome – sometimes within the Church as well as outside it – is the belief that the moral teaching of the Church lacks compassion. There is a widespread perception that pastoral compassion lies in opposition to orthodox moral teaching, especially on pro-life issues.

We might actually say that this perception is applied principally to pro-life issues. Few people would imagine that we should not preach about honesty because one or two of our parishioners have done time for robbery. If we have written one of those priest's letters to the court saying that young John is very sorry he got in the fight, that he is a good boy really, has learnt his lesson and will benefit from a non-custodial sentence, we do not thereby feel constrained not to preach about the sin of anger.

Of course, it is true that pro-life issues affect people very deeply. However the evidence very clearly shows that STIs have risen sharply over the past ten years in our country where contraception is widely promoted. When people find that out, will they consider us compassionate for never having mentioned the teaching of the Church?

Abortion

If people receive the impression from the media that the Church has an unforgiving and condemnatory attitude towards women who have had an abortion, will they consider us compassionate for never having read to them Pope John Paul's words to women who have had an abortion?

> I would now like to say a special word to *women who have had an abortion*. The Church is aware of the many factors which may have influenced your decision, and she does not doubt that in many cases it was a painful and even shattering decision. The wound in your heart may not yet have healed. Certainly what happened was and remains terribly wrong. But do not give in to discouragement and do not lose hope. Try rather to understand what happened and face it honestly. If you have not already done so, give yourselves over with humility and trust to repentance. The Father of mercies is ready to give you his forgiveness and his peace in the Sacrament of Reconciliation. You will come to understand that nothing is definitively lost and you will also be able to ask forgiveness from your child, who is now living in the Lord. With the friendly and expert help and advice of other people, and as a result of your own painful experience, you can be among the most eloquent defenders of everyone's right to life. Through your commitment to life, whether by accepting the birth of other children or by welcoming and caring for those

most in need of someone to be close to them, you will become promoters of a new way of looking at human life.[65]

For many clergy, it is a matter of regaining confidence. People need to hear this message. We are used to being compassionate in various situations and can approach these matters with the appropriate sensitivity without masking the truth. It is also a matter of pastoral compassion to ensure that our people do know the truth.[66] We live in a country that has killed 6 million of its own inhabitants by abortion. Will be be able to face a future generation that wakes up to these horrors and asks us "What did you do?"

Euthanasia

Our country is also beginning to kill the elderly and the disabled through euthanasia. An important point to make to people is that this is already happening. The morality of the withdrawal of food and fluids is not a matter of splitting hairs. It makes all the difference whether you are discontinuing an invasive or burdensome treatment or withdrawing food and fluids with the intention of ending someone's life. Hospital chaplains and most parish clergy will know of the increasing worry that families have over the treatment of their elderly relatives.

Regarding euthanasia, we need to counter the media-driven prejudice that the Church wishes to subject the elderly to a slow and agonising death. The truth is that the slow and agonising death will be more common if food and fluids are withdrawn. This state of affairs is unlikely to last for very long. The "inconvenience" of it will be all too apparent and the morphine syringe driver is already widely available. All that is necessary is to change its use from the proper relief of pain (and usually therefore the prolonging of a life) and to utilise the same technology as a means of killing.

We are just beginning to see the emergence of attitudes that are current in Holland where the elderly are frightened to go to hospital.

---

[65] Pope John Paul II *Evangelium Vitae* (1995) n.99.
[66] Cf. Fr Frank Pavone *Preaching about abortion online* at www.priestsforlife.org/preaching/preach.html (Accessed 21/11/06).

The provision of truthful information and simply presented sound moral teaching is a vital part of our pastoral ministry to our people.

Protection of the embryo

One of the obstacles to convincing people of the value of the embryo is that it appears that here we are actually just dealing with a clump of cells. This is not in fact the case as Fr John Fleming eloquently demonstrated in a lecture given at one of the SPUC Clergy Information Days. From the beginning, the very first cell, there is differentiation which is vital for the development of the human body and its organs.

I have found that the example of Christ the embryo is a powerful way to speak to Christian people about the importance of the embryo. As I wrote in the last issue of the APGL Briefing, the Visitation,

> ... shows Elizabeth and the infant John the Baptist responding to the presence of Jesus Christ only a few days after his conception. At this stage in his life, as an embryo whose cells can still be counted easily, Jesus Christ is recognised as truly God and truly man.

Our people can also readily appreciate that the manufacture of human life is abhorrent. They can accept that life cannot be treated as a disposable commodity to be manipulated. We should also reflect with them on the effect of this industry on future generations. The instruction *Donum Vitae*, in addition to considering other aspects of the morality of various techniques of human reproduction, focussed particularly on the right of a person in respect of the manner in which they were conceived. It spoke of "the right of every person to be conceived and to be born within marriage and from marriage."[67] With regard to homologous artificial fertilisation[68] the instruction said,

---

[67] Congregation for the Doctrine of the Faith, Instruction *Donum Vitae* (1987) I.6

[68] That is, *in vitro* fertilisation, embryo transfer, and artificial insemination between husband and wife; as distinct from the use of sperm or embryos that come from people other than the couple themselves.

Challenges and Opportunities in Pro-Life Preaching

No one may subject the coming of a child into the world to conditions of technical efficiency which are to be evaluated according to standards of control and dominion. The moral relevance of the link between the meanings of the conjugal act and between the goods of marriage, as well as the unity of the human being and the dignity of his origin, demand that the procreation of a human person be brought about as the fruit of the conjugal act specific to the love between spouses.[69]

The Church considers not only the moral evaluation of artificial fertilisation from the point of view of the principle of the non-separation of the procreative and unitive aspects of marriage in principle, it also considers the reasons for this principle and the consequences of transgressing it. In this case, such consequences would include the possible traumatic discovery by a young person that their conception was not the fruit of the conjugal act but the result of a laboratory procedure.

Opportunities within the Church
New growth of faith among the young

Within the pro-life movement, we need to be aware of the many opportunities presented by what Cardinal Pell has called the John Paul II generation. Older priests and teachers sometimes make the mistake of thinking that the one danger to be avoided is "indoctrination" and that young people need to be presented with a choice of views to evaluate. Young people themselves, on the other hand, are increasingly open to discovering the manner in which they have been the subjects of indoctrination by the traditional media.

Young people who are continuing to practice their faith do so against pressure from their peers and widespread propaganda. The come to Church because they have decided to do so. They are open to hearing the fullness of the Catholic faith and are eager for clear teaching on how to defend it.

---

[69] *Donum Vitae* II.4c.

This is particularly true of moral issues, especially those related to the pro-life cause. In some cases, they will suffer violent opposition from pro-abortion activists at university or on the street when they take part in pro-life vigils. The history of the Church leaves us in no doubt about the effect of persecution on the fervour of young Catholics.

Young parents

The present generation of young parents is also increasingly open to hearing sound teaching on pro-life matters. They are the remnant of what one priest aptly described as the "condoning generation." Their own parents were often silent about the morality of abortion and contraception, or made an exception to the teaching when it meant any possible stigma or disgrace to their own family. They can see where it has led, they know that there is something deeply wrong with a society that assumes that 13 year olds will be sexually active and that primary age children must be taught about homosexuality.

They also know that they know nothing. Often, they will freely admit that they understand very little about their faith. They will be unembarrassed about this and rightly so. It is not their fault but the fault of the Church for having failed to fulfil its responsibility to educate them when they were young.

They need us to spell out for them the reasonable nature of the Church's teaching, its promotion of the dignity of the human person, and its consistent opposition to the currents of thought that have led to the current disastrous consequences of sexual immorality in our country.

The education and formation of parents is another vast opportunity that we have hardly begun to address. From my own experience, I would also say that it is an opportunity to revitalise our parishes. When young parents understand the cultural battle in which we are engaged, they will become more involved in parish life, whether actively in the pro-life movement or simply in other areas of parish life that help us to keep the parish afloat.

Challenges and Opportunities in Pro-Life Preaching

Young clergy

Many pro-life laity who have been campaigning for many years have become jaded with the lack of support, or even outright hostility that they receive from many Catholic priests. I never tire of encouraging them to seek out our fine young clergy. These men, ordained in recent years, are for the most part enthusiastic in their active support of and work for the pro-life cause. Indeed, the pro-life movement is itself a fertile seedbed for vocations.

This is a part of the phenomenon of the John Paul II generation. Nowadays, nobody is going to become a priest in order to change the Church's teaching. There is obviously no likelihood of the Church wavering on celibacy or changing its teaching on contraception. These young clergy know this and went to the seminary knowing it. Wholeheartedly in support of the teaching of the Magisterium, they are eager to evangelise and particularly eager to preach the Gospel of Life. If you are tempted to despair of the future of the Church, get to know them and your depression will be cured.

Oportunities within the culture
Growing suspicion of the media

Within our culture too, I believe that there are now opportunities for the promotion of the pro-life message that did not exist even a few years ago.

Among ordinary people, a "media literacy" has led to growing suspicion of the traditional media and disillusionment with it. This is an opportunity that we can exploit because we have known for some years that such suspicion and disillusionment is very well founded. We can reinforce the suspicion by clearly pointing out examples of misinformation and bias. If we do this often enough, our people can become inoculated to a large degree against its automatic influence. We should not underestimate our ability to fight back against the propaganda of the traditional media.

My people now come to tell me when they saw something that wasn't really too bad in its analysis of some life or family issue. I have no mercy. I ask them why we should be grateful that the media occasionally manage to broadcast half the truth instead of vicious anti-life propaganda.

Growing use of new media

In addition, there is a vast opportunity for us in the growing use of the new media, especially the internet. By using such media ourselves, it is possible for us to set the agenda, to present information attractively, to mediate the traditional media and fight against anti-life propaganda on something more like a level playing field.

If you are not familiar with these developments, perhaps a couple of statistics will help to indicate the importance of these developments. AsiaMedia reported last month that:

Members of the 13-24 age group are each spending 17 hours on average every week on the internet, according to a study by US research firms Harris Interactive and Teenage Research Unlimited in June. The same group's members each spend 14 hours a week watching television.[70]

In April of this year, I began writing a "blog." That is to say a kind of online diary in which I can write text, and post pictures or videos. It is free and I can write whatever I want. I can also link to other sources of information on the internet. A meter checks how many people visit the blog each day. Since 22nd April, there have been 46,000 visitors and the current 30 day moving average stands at about 450 visitors per day. This is modest compared to some American Catholic blogs that have several thousand visitors per day. It is easy to see how this is a powerful way in which to influence opinion – all the time subverting the traditional media or bypassing it entirely.

Wealth of information and research

A further opportunity is the wealth of information and research that is available to us. We should not neglect the studies that have been produced by the various departments of the Holy See. The

---

[70] AsiaMedia article, *US: Old media told to build Web alliances* Online at asiamedia.ucla.edu/article-us.asp?parentid=56668 (Accessed 21/11/06).

Pontifical Council for the Family, the Pontifical Academy for Life, and the Pontifical Council for Health and Pastoral Care, produce excellent analyses of various moral questions.

Pro-Life organisations also provide a wealth of information. SPUC, the Linacre Centre, Human Life International, and Priests for Life, to name just a few, produce good quality information, well researched and easily available. I know that priests sometimes complain about the amount of mail that they receive from pro-life groups but you can be sure that if you need assistance on any important pro-life question, it is probably already out there.

The dissemination of this information is also greatly helped by the internet which makes it possible to search a vast repository of pro-life material. In addition, there are excellent sites such as Life Site News, or SPUC's daily bulletin and their service providing links to Hansard for life-related Parliamentary answers and Parliamentary proceedings.

We have never had so much easily available information to assist us in the pro-life cause. We should not exaggerate the difficulty of assimilating this information because it is now so easy to obtain specific information on any topic with which we are particularly concerned.

Consistent Pro-Life ethic

In our preaching, we aim to change hearts and minds and by that means to change lives. In preaching the Gospel of Life, we cannot make any separation of the various issues we are faced with. I find Fr John Pavone's expression "the consistent pro-life ethic" helpful.

We have always known that the promotion of contraception leads to abortion as a backup solution where the contraception fails. The massive growth of STIs and the growing awareness that many of the abortions in our hospitals, and many indeed of the live births, happen despite the fact that the couple concerned were using one of the various forms of contraception.

Sex-education in schools that promotes the use of contraception inevitably also promotes the use of the Morning After Pill and promotes the availability of abortion.

Conversely, the promotion of chastity leads to young people becoming more at home with their natural abhorrence of abortion. Chastity naturally leads to an appreciation of human fertility, and of Natural Family Planning, whether used in order to achieve conception or to avoid it for the time being. Families who use NFP often have a larger number of children: not because they have failed to avoid conception but because the use of NFP has itself drawn them to reconsider their decision not to have another child.

If we wish to promote the family and to safeguard its stability, we would do well to remember that the divorce rate among couples who use NFP is less than a tenth that of couples who contracept. (This is yet another example of how the truth is also pastorally compassionate.)

We will find that the promotion of chastity will meet with vehement approval from parents once their consciousness is raised concerning the appalling assault on the innocence of their children that is perpetrated in the name of sex-education.

But will anybody listen?

After all this, some clergy will still say to us that nobody will listen. We should not be so lacking in confidence. The first papal condemnation of modern slavery was published in 1492, the year of Columbus' famous voyage to the New World. Papal teaching was ignored for centuries and parish priests neglected to preach it. Yet who now would say that the Popes were anything but right on this issue?

Similarly, the Popes forbade duelling. Their teaching was ignored by nobles who continued to duel. The Popes continued to preach in season and out of season. Yet now, nobody would support duelling.

Pope Paul was vilified for *Humanae Vitae*. During the week after his death, an English newspaper columnist accused Pope John Paul of having the blood of millions on his hands,[71] ultimately because of his preaching of the Gospel of Life. As with slavery and duelling, it

---

[71] Terry Eagleton "The Pope has blood on his hands" *Guardian* 4th April 2005. See also Polly Toynbee "Not in my name" *Guardian* 8th April 2005. The cover story for the *New Statesman* that week carried a similar message.

may take many years before people realise the evil that our society perpetrates in its promotion of the culture of death. That is no reason for priests to neglect preaching the Gospel of Life today.

Contributors

The role of the priest in promoting the Gospel of Life
Mgr Ignacio Barreiro served in the Uruguayan Foreign Service before entering the priesthood. He is currently Director of the Rome office of Human life International, actively supporting Pro-life campaigns in many different parts of the world. He was appointed a Chaplain of His Holiness in 2004.

Vatian II, Culture and the Gospel of Life
Fr Aidan Nichols is a member of the Order of Preachers (Dominicans). Author of many theological books and articles he has held the first lectureship in Catholic theology Oxford University since the Reformation, and was formerly Prior of St Michael and All Angels, Cambridge.

Pope Pius XII and the Gospel of Life
Fr John Saward is Parish Priest of SS Gregory and Augustine, Oxford, and was formerly Professor of Dogmatic Theology at the International Theological Institute, Gaming. He has written widely on theological and spiritual themes and has been responsible for the English translations of works by Hans Urs Von Balthasar, Pope Benedict XVI and Cardinal Christoph Schonborn.

Challenges and opportunities in pro-life preaching
Fr Timothy Finigan is the founder of the Association of Priests for the Gospel of Life. He is Parish Priest of Our Lady of the Rosary, Blackfen, and a Visiting Lecturer in Sacramental Theology at St John's Seminary, Wonersh. He runs the well-known weblog, 'The Hermeneutic of Continuity'.

What is Association of Priests for the Gospel of Life?

The Association of Priests for the Gospel of Life was founded in June 2004 by Fr Timothy Finigan. It is a response to the insistent call of Pope John Paul II to preach the Gospel of Life in our modern world. The APLG seeks to provide a service to Catholic priests with regard to the particular challenges we face in the United Kingdom at the present day.

Understanding the particular duty of the priest to preach the truth of the Gospel 'in season and out of season' (2 *Tm* 4:5), and recognising the many difficulties priests find in exercising this ministry today, the APGL seeks to unite and encourage priests and to offer them support in the pro-life aspects of their priestly ministry.

The aims and objectives of the APGL

As a part of the priestly life to offer prayer, sacrifice and witness to promote the Gospel of Life. Members undertake to offer one Mass each year for the protection of human life.

To support, encourage and where appropriate, advise lay Catholics who are involved with pro-life activity.

To keep priests informed about legal, social and scientific developments in the field of pro-life activity.

To provide a network for priests involved in pro-life work or interested in becoming more involved.

To proclaim the Gospel of Life in our parishes and in the media. To offer help to those facing crisis pregnancies or end-of-life dilemmas.